THE INTERSECTION OF FAITH, MIGRATION AND GOD'S MISSION

A call for the people of God in the West to engage in Mission Dei

ERIC TANGUMONKEM, PH.D.

IEM PRESS (PO Box 831001, Richardson, TX 75080) functions only as book publisher. As such, the ultimate design, content, editorial accuracy, and views expressed or implied in this work are those of the author. No part of this publication may be reproduced, stored in a retrieval system, or transmitted in any way by any means—electronic, mechanical, photocopy, recording, or otherwise—without the prior permission of the copyright holder, except as provided by USA copyright law. Unless otherwise noted, all Scriptures are taken from the Holy Bible, New International Version®, NIV®. Copyright © 1973, 1978, 1984, 2011 by Biblica, Inc.™ Used by permission of Zondervan. All rights reserved worldwide. www. zondervan.com ISBN

ISBN: 978-1-947662-60-5

Library of Congress Catalog Card Number: 2019954585

That delivers us from bondage
    To the world that once ensnared;
Oh, the coming of the Kingdom draweth near.
    Oh, the world is growing weary,
        It has waited now so long;
And the hearts of men are failing them for fear.
    Let us tell them of the Kingdom;
        Let us cheer them with the song,
That the coming of the Kingdom draweth near.
    Oh, the coming of the Kingdom draweth near,
    Oh, the coming of the Kingdom draweth near:
        Be thou ready, my soul,
        For the trumpet soon may roll,
    And the King in His glory shall appear.

Tables of Contents

Table of Contents

Dedication

To all brave participants of the Mission Dei in the West

FORWARD:

The Hope of the world, which includes the United States of America, is in our Lord Jesus Christ

Dr. Tangumonkem's book, *The Intersection of Faith, Migration and God's Mission,* is a timely, clarion call to Western Christians: "It is time to take off the Conservative cover, the Democrat cover, the Republican cover, the Tea Party cover, the Libertarian cover or whatever cover you have on and let the light of God shine through us."

Whereas this is a pinnacle statement in this outstanding book, it is opposed by the politicizing of the Gospel by much of the church in the West. The Church's politicizing of the Gospel — that is, delivering the Gospel under the cover of Democrat, Republican, Tea Party, Libertarian "or whatever" — has resulted in the church "taking sides" in our nation's currently polarized state.

But rather than taking our cues on immigration from the hysteria of present-day politics or the media, believers urgently need to hear what the Spirit has to say to the Church — The mission field, formerly removed far from our shore in distant lands has come to us!

And because we ourselves are partakers of eternal life through faith in Jesus Christ, we must engage the weak, the vulnerable and the disenfranchised now among us with the Gospel — "The condition of their soul should be our paramount concern because we have found the source of life and are partakers of that life," is a theme consistently stressed by Eric throughout this book.

Dr. Tangumonkem's argument is indeed seasoned with salt, and illuminated by the light of the Gospel, but it is not one-dimensional, it is multi-layered and marked by cogent wisdom and the insight of a scholar, an African immigrant, a proud [legalized] American citizen and a man possessing reverence for the law of the land.

The Western Church must understand that the myriad of socio-political problems, to include immigration, presently confronting America, are pre-political. And therefore, the church must be aware that because "... the demographics of the type of immigrants that we are receiving is changing rapidly, we cannot afford not to reach them with the Gospel and help them transition into the American life and become part of the country." Assimilation through the hope of the indestructible Gospel of Jesus Christ is a great moral responsibility of the church — This contention forms a foundational layer in Eric's book.

Three major biblical themes punctuated the sixteenth-century Reformation: *Sola Scriptura* — Biblical Revelation alone is the authority for all teaching and moral action throughout the kingdom of God; Justification is by faith alone, through grace alone in Christ alone and the priesthood of all believers.

Another layer of this outstanding book involves the missional journey of the church — *mission Dei* (God's Mission). The church effectively joins the mission of God through the priesthood of all believers — *Through faith in Jesus Christ, all believers are a part of the priesthood of believers* (1 Peter 2:4-5; 9/Rev. 1:6). *How do believers perform as priests? They join Jesus in His mission and through their daily work and lives, they minister to people in their work environments (and lives in general) by doing the works God prepared for them to do before the creation of the cosmos* (et. al., Eph. 2:10).

Eric is a voice in the wilderness crying out for the body of Christ to come together and be who they really are — the light and salt of the earth. Therefore, "whatever decision the politicians make, our attitude towards both the legal and illegal immigrant population should not change":

We should love people enough to tell those who are illegal, those who have willfully broken American immigration laws or the laws of any other country that it is wrong to break laws because lawlessness harms everybody. We cannot be afraid to call people to order under the pretext of justice and love. What are we going to tell those that pay the price to obey the laws and do what is right? How is this fair to them? Let us love enough to challenge people to develop the moral character to do what is right because people of character and moral rectitude benefit themselves and the rest of society in the long run.

This book is a clear, compelling and sane message that people, especially believers, need to hear: "We are people who love God and love our neighbors as ourselves."

Kerry "Mac" McRoberts

Dean, The School of Missional Practice, Missional University

N. Augusta, South Carolina

November 7, 2019

Introduction

If you watch television, Google the Internet, or read some of the news headlines, then you know about global migration, specifically of people from less developed countries moving to developed countries for greener pastures. This massive movement of people is made possible by the airplane and other faster transportation modes. This phenomenon has no end in sight. It will only increase as the world population continues to increase, and the gap between the rich countries and poorer countries gets wider.

What has this got to do with you or the Mission Dei? I believe it has everything to do with you and Mission Dei because you are an ambassador of the kingdom of heaven, and your main responsibility is to align yourself with what God is doing right now. You already know that the number one thing on God's mind is to reconcile the world to Him through our Lord Jesus Christ, and you have a vital part to play in this process. God has positioned you where you are right now for this purpose, and every other thing is secondary.

With this movement of people comes advantages and some serious challenges that must be addressed as soon as possible. Most countries are not adequately equipped to handle this large migration of people. Therefore, many buried their heads in the sand and pretended that there is no problem. Others pray for the problem to go away because they do not want to deal with it. Some strengthen their national defenses, hoping to keep the intruders out.

The purpose of this book is not to put anybody on the spot, but to call upon the people of God to rise up and be the light and salt Jesus Christ our Lord, Savior, and Master has made us be. He left us on earth to do just that, and we have to start in the area of welcoming the stranger and being one another's keeper. God is bringing to us the people that our sons, daughters, husbands, and wives travel thousands of miles to go and share the Gospel with. We loved these people in all these far-away foreign lands so much that we were willing to sacrifice all to share the love of God with them. God is bringing them to us for a reason, and we should embrace that.

The present political climate and rhetoric are making it extremely difficult, if not impossible, for us to have a level-headed discussion when it comes to this topic of migration. It is unfortunate that the people of God have been caught up in this and are divided on what to do as well. Nobody said it was going to be easy, but we are light, and where there is darkness, we must stand up and let our light shine. We cannot hide our light under nationalistic tendencies or political correctness. Now is the time for the people of God to stand up firmly and speak the truth in love.

We, the bride of Jesus Christ, are aliens, strangers, and pilgrims on earth, and we are following in the footsteps of our Master, who left heaven to come here on earth. When a wicked and evil king wanted to kill Him, He went to Egypt as an immigrant and only returned when King Herod died. What would have happened if there was no Egypt for Him to run to? We know the Egyptians were hospitable because there is no report of Joseph, Mary, and the baby Jesus suffering persecution, discrimination or segregation, of any sort. In fact, God asked them to go down to Egypt.

Has it occurred to you that some of the immigrants have been asked by God to move to where they are right now? If you doubt that, remember that God asked Abraham to move and asked Jacob and his family to move as well. Has it occurred to you that some of these immigrants are fleeing from wicked and evil rulers who have made life unbearable, even killing their own people? It is sad that most people do not reflect enough to understand the root cause of people moving from one part of the world to another.

The purpose of writing this book is to highlight the opportunities that migration brings and that immigrants are not a liability, but a resource with immense untapped potential. The call is for the people of God to take the lead in ensuring that this great potential is tapped and positioned for the advancement of the kingdom of God and God's mission for this generation. We, the people of God, must get out of our walls and comfort zones and begin to engage those that God is bringing into our communities.

God works in mysterious ways. The people of God in the West sent thousands of missionaries to "heathen" countries to bring the Good News of salvation to them and to proclaim God's unconditional love to all people. Today, God is bringing the world to western Europe, to the United States of America, and to other developed countries. Many people are freaking out about it. By the end of this book, your fear and frustration will be transformed into a passion for reaching out to these immigrants and making a difference in their lives.

You are an immigrant not because your grandparents migrated; it is because you are a citizen of heaven, and your kingdom is not of this world. Many of us forget the reason we are here, and this hampers us from fulfilling our call to love God with our heart and love our neighbor as ourselves. This is the entire Gospel, and we cannot afford to continue doing our own thing and living the way we deem fit. We have to desire to please God and follow that desire by action.

We cannot love God and not love people. Love and hate are mutually exclusive. We, the people of God who are beneficiaries of God's unconditional love, can love other people, including immigrants. It is high time the people of God wake up from their slumber and take the lead for others to follow. We should not allow the government to pass laws to teach us to do what our Master has already commanded us to do. We are called to love and to love all people. God's love is universal, and we have that love in us. Therefore, we should extend that love to those that God is bringing into our countries. It is imperative for the people of God, wherever they are, to see what He is already doing and get along with the program. We have what it takes to show those who are not walking in the light how to really walk in the light. We have the light of God in us, and we have the capacity to shine that light in a world full of darkness. Light has always overcome darkness, and it is not going to fail in our generation.

Some may already be suspicious about the call to love and embrace immigrants. Do not let the fear-driven propaganda of people coming over and taking over your country to cause you to listen to what God is already doing. I will say up front that I am not for open borders and unchecked immigration. People will have to respect the laws of the countries in which they move into and be law-abiding. This is not just a call for people to move without being considerate and respectful of the country they want help from. We who are strong have to show compassion and love to the vulnerable. If these people were valuable enough for us to sacrifice the lives of our sons and daughters to reach them, we have to show the same level of love and sacrifice to reach them now that they are coming to us. We need to engage them and show them the love of God. We cannot afford to be indifferent because the price the society will pay is too high, and there will be eternal ramifications.

There is a need for us to have this conversation now because a lot of people from different parts of the world have already moved into the United States of America for greener pastures and are pursuing the American dream. This has led to fear among some of the citizens who view these immigrants as a potential source of problems within the country.

One of the solutions is to build a wall and keep these people out. A wall will keep some of them out, but what about those who are already here and are not being assimilated? As somebody put it, "Just because you show up on the shores of America, you do not automatically become an American." There is a need for immigrants to learn how to get assimilated into the American way of life.

According to some people, using the word "assimilation" is offensive because it means that somebody has to lose something, or insinuates that some people are not good enough. The call for immigrants to assimilate has nothing to do with their character or their worth. The fundamental question that needs to be asked by all is, "Why did the people leave their country of birth, and why did they choose to move to the United States of America?" This is a legitimate question, and it is not racially motivated. The answer to this question will determine the next plan of action.

If somebody says they moved because their country of birth failed them economically and they chose the UNITED STATES OF AMERICA because the economy is good, then they must know that the UNITED STATES OF AMERICA economy is good because of some reasons. The economy is not operating in a vacuum. It is following some principles, and those who move to America must understand what these principles are and adhere to them. Why? These immigrants had a set of values and principles that they operated by when they were in their country of origin, and if their country's principles failed, there is no need to repeat them in the UNITED STATES OF AMERICA.

Common sense teaches us that if you do the same thing and expect to get different results, you are self-delusional, to say the least. I write this as an immigrant myself and have nothing against other immigrants, but it does not make sense to insist on changing America to become like that place you fled from. There is so much talk about diversity and inclusion. But many do not see the fallacy in insisting that people who have migrated from failed countries should not be challenged, encouraged, and helped to adopt new ways that have been proven to deliver.

This is not an attempt to rank countries or judge people in any way; it is speaking the truth for what it is. If a person's country of origin met their needs, he/she would not move to a different country. How many Americans migrate to different countries? A few do. Why? Because their country is delivering for them. Demanding that immigrants fit in is not a bad idea. It is the right thing to do, and it will benefit everybody. It is not an easy process, and it is tempting to take the path of least resistance and just allow the immigrants to their own devices. This will bring many undesirable consequences and will transform the country in a way that the current residents will not like. There is no need to live in fear of what is going to happen. Now is the time to rise up and engage the immigrants and ensure that they are equipped with what it is going to take to make them successful citizens of their new country.

Wishing that the immigrants were not here is a little too late.

They are already here and are having children, and their numbers are increasing. The best thing to do is to learn how to engage them. Do not allow false guilt to prevent you from doing what you know is the right thing to do.

The purpose of this book is to show you how to go about this important and crucial task. This is a book from the perspective of an immigrant who has lived in the UNITED STATES OF AMERICA for over fifteen years and has firsthand knowledge of where the shoes pinch and what must be done to alleviate the pain. We cannot allow fear and ignorance to drive the agenda because we know that knowledge is the best antidote for fear.

This book is for those in the household of God who have been bought by the blood of the Lamb and truly understand what it means to love God and to love their neighbors as themselves. I am going to get very practical and down-to-earth on what is supposed to be done by the people of God in the UNITED STATES OF AMERICA and other developed countries who are experiencing an influx of immigrants. The other crucial part is going to be understanding why this must be done. The price of not doing anything is too high, and we cannot afford it.

The purpose of this book is not to blame or condemn the people of God in developed countries or place them on a guilt trip. It is a call for them to rise up and be the body of Christ as the Master Himself intended it to be. The people of God must step up and engage those that God has brought to them because this is the right thing to do. If the people of God do not do this heavy lifting, who else is going to do it? We cannot rely on the government to legislate whom we should love and treat as strangers among us. We, the people of God, understand our role and must do it because it is pleasing to our heavenly Father.

I am writing as a fellow pilgrim, alien, and stranger who has moved to the UNITED STATES OF AMERICA more than fifteen years ago. Over the years, I have witnessed and encountered some of the issues that will be addressed in the book. We are one body, one family, and belong to the household of God, especially those believers that God is prompting from different parts of the globe to move to the UNITED STATES OF AMERICA and other western countries. We in the West sent out missionaries, and now God is sending the mission to us. It is crucial that we start viewing these brothers and sisters in this light and opening up to them. This is not an easy task, but we cannot shy away from it. We must obey God, not man, and not our culture. We are expected to go about our Father's business and should not allow anything to distract us from that.

This is a message to the people of God in the West, especially in the **UNITED STATES OF AMERICA,** where I have had the privilege of living and interacting for the past fifteen plus years. There is going to be no attempt to polish the message or make it politically correct. We should not mention political correctness among God's people, but unfortunately, we live in a time where many people have made their own god in their own image and likeness, and they will do all to fit in and not cause any disturbance. Pleasing people is done at all costs, and a lot of resources are invested in improving their likeability factor. People are more terrified of what other people will say about them than what God says.

You can read this book in any order, but to get the most out of it, you may follow the suggested outline. Many of you may be wondering how to reach out to those who are here in the **UNITED STATES OF AMERICA** but are not originally from here. There are two categories of immigrants: those who are believers in the Lord Jesus Christ and those who are not. Therefore, it is going to take different approaches to engage these two groups. This book will equip you with how to do that.

The ideas that I will present and discuss are simple enough, but you may be wondering why these simple ideas are not being implemented. We all know that faith without works is dead. Unfortunately, most people quote this scripture but never obey it.

One other aspect of this book is the call to ask tough questions that necessitate some personal changes. You may not be aware that there is a need for a change in the present state-of-affairs. Hopefully, this will be a wake-up call for you, and you will answer the call to action. The time has passed for us to use our culture, personal comfort, or traditions as excuses for not loving as God commands us to. The world is watching us, and we cannot continue to cover our light and keep our salt in the shaker. It is time to take off the Conservative cover, the Democrat cover, the Republican cover, the Tea Party cover, the Libertarian cover, or whatever cover you have on and let the light of God shine through us.

There is nothing wrong with being any of these things, but they should never take precedence over our identity in Christ. We are, first and foremost, the children of God, ambassadors of the kingdom of heaven, pilgrims, aliens, and strangers on this earth. If we believe these truths, we must live them as well. The time to pay lip service to who we truly are is over. It is the time to recognize that a lost, decaying world needs us to stand up and preserve it. A world where people are stumbling in darkness needs us to shine our light so that they can see where they are going. Are you ready to be that light and salt? Then, let us get into the book and grow together.

Chapter 1:
Why Me?

There is nothing wrong with asking God, "Why me?" Many in the past have asked that question, directly or indirectly. Take the case of Moses. When God showed up in the burning bush and asked him to go back to Egypt and free the children of Israel from bondage, he reacted in a way that is typical of many humans. "Lord, send somebody else. I do not have what it takes. Have You forgotten that I have flaws?" He was concerned about his speech impediment. How could Moses think that God was not aware of his past liabilities and present challenges and flaws? When God initiates, He knows the past, the present, and the future. We must trust Him with our past, present, and future. Needless to say, we all know that God did not back down because Moses complained. God had chosen His man for the assignment, and Moses was not going to explain or complain his way out of it.

Another example of somebody who felt that God was out of His mind for calling him to go on a divine mission is the prophet, Jonah. God instructed him to go to the city of Nineveh and warn them of God's impending judgment if they did not repent from their evil ways. This instruction did not make any sense to Jonah, or he felt that the people of Nineveh deserved the wrath of God to fall upon them. Therefore, there was no point in him obeying God and going there to deliver the message. In Jonah's mind, God had forgotten the evil that the Ninevites had committed against the child of Israel. It was payback time, and he was not going to have anything to do with any message of grace and forgiveness. Jonah was so adamant that he did the unthinkable: he decided to run away from God and go to Joppa, a city that was in the opposite direction from Nineveh.

Most of us are not different from Jonah. We do the unthinkable because we'd rather stay in our comfort zone and do what comes naturally to us than do anything that would make us go against the popular culture. Just like the case of Moses, God was not going to let a mere mortal act with impunity. He had chosen Jonah for the mission, and Jonah and nobody else was going to deliver that message. God would do everything in His power to ensure that His mission was accomplished. Jonah had to spend three days in the belly of a fish for some sense to be knocked into him.

You do not have to wait for God to knock some sense into you for you to get on board with God's mission. This mission is so important to God that He was willing to sacrifice His one and only Son for it. God takes this seriously, for He has already invested in it heavily. What are you waiting for? Do you want God to speak again after the instructions have clearly been given?

The question should be, "Why not me?" This should be followed by the affirmation, "Send me, Lord, and I will go." And it should be accompanied by, "Whatever you want me to do, I am available. Use me, Lord." Unfortunately, many wish things had not changed because the good old days are forever lost. They are confused as to why there is a sudden influx of people into this country from places they cannot even pronounce or even identify on the map. These immigrants are coming in with strange accents, beliefs, cultures, and customs that do not fit the American way. In some people's minds, this influx of people is going to ruin the country and change it into something they will not be able to recognize.

One of the greatest fears of some is the possibility that some of these immigrants will get married to their children, and the thought of it makes some recoil in horror. This has led some to ask, "Why me, Lord? Why do I have to be the one to deal with these people? Can't things just return to normal?" I have a question for you. If not you, who else do you want God to use to advance His kingdom here on earth? Do you think any of this is happening without God's knowledge? Do you think God is unaware? Do you think that God does not know who you are, where you are, and the difficulties and challenges you are facing?

God is still on the throne, 100 percent in control, and is aware of what is going on. Has it occurred to you that maybe God seems far off because you are praying the wrong prayer? Instead of asking for wisdom to engage and let God use you to establish His kingdom in the lives of these immigrants, you are praying for God to stop them from coming in and for those who are already here to stay in their own corner and do their own thing. It is time to trust God to turn what the enemy has meant for bad, for the good of this greatest country on earth.

The influx of people into the UNITED STATES OF AMERICA has many different explanations that we are going to look at, but as a person of faith, never forget that sin is the root cause. The solution to sin is the Lord Jesus Christ. Therefore, you have the solution because you have accepted the Lord Jesus Christ as your Lord and Savior, and He is living inside of you.

Would you have preferred to be sent off to some foreign country thousands of miles away to share the Gospel to people who may want to kill you? You make your pick because God is not going to let you sit idly doing nothing. Remember that in the past, thousands of young American men and women were sent to foreign mission fields. Many of these people gave up the comforts, security, and the pleasures of home to fulfill God's mission. Many of them went through untold suffering and sacrifices to share the love of God with strangers. At times, some of these missionaries were trying to reach people who were not interested in what they had to share. In other places, they were not welcomed at all and were chased out of their countries. Some of these missionaries had to make the ultimate sacrifice of laying down their lives.

There is nothing glamorous about being brutally beaten to death or being shot and dumped in a river to be eaten by crocodiles. Most of the bodies of these brethren were not recovered and given proper funerals. They had no time to say goodbye to their loved ones. They had no time to hug their children, wives, husbands, and parents for the last time. They died among strangers without anybody to comfort or encourage them. They were abused, downtrodden, and humiliated for doing good.

We thank God for the bravery of these men and women, and all they allowed God to do through them. We are not minimizing the work that present-day missionaries are doing all over the world. Many are still being imprisoned, tortured, insulted, and killed for the sake of the Gospel. At times, these fellow brothers and sisters in Christ are raising their children under primitive conditions, with the risk of malaria and other diseases. Do not say that the money that you give to support these brave and courageous brethren is all that is needed from you. All the resources God has entrusted you with belong to Him 100 percent, and you have to let God use them, including your life. The mission field that was "out there" is nowhere, and we cannot afford not to engage.

These stories were not brought up to make you feel guilty or put you down in any way. It is a reminder of what it takes to participate in the Mission Dei. You do not need to travel thousands of miles to preach the Gospel to some "heathens" who do not care about what you have to say. You are being called to go out of your neighborhood and your social circle to reach out to people that are hungry for what this greatest country on earth has to offer. Most of the immigrants are here because they believe that the UNITED STATES OF AMERICA has a lot to offer. They are here for the American dream, and we should tell them there is a place that is a trillion times better, a place that cannot be compared to the UNITED STATES OF AMERICA or any other western country. We have to be bold enough to say that everything that we see and have is temporal and will sooner or later pass away, but our eternal home is forever established by God Himself and will never be moved. This is not in any way saying that we must ignore what's on earth and only focus on the heavenly. It is a call for us to put things in the right perspective and prioritize what is eternally important.

You may still be wondering, "Why me?" Who else do you want God to use? Have you forgotten that you are not your own and have been bought at a price?

Do you not know that your bodies are temples of the Holy Spirit, who is in you, whom you have received from God? You are not your own; you were bought at a price. Therefore, honor God with your bodies. (1 Corinthians 6:19-20 NIV)

Although the context in which this was written has to do with how we use our bodies, it was still extended to other things, including how we use our time and resources. The emphasis here is on the fact that you were bought, and you are no longer your own. When you buy anything, you become the owner and do with it as you please because you paid the price for it. We, too, have been bought by the price Jesus Christ paid on the cross through His death. Therefore, we belong to God 100 percent and cannot do as we please. We are no longer our own, and God has ownership of our time and resources. The good news is that God loves us and has our best interest at heart. He will never ask us to do anything He has not equipped us to do.

The other reason why you are the person to carry out God's mission is the fact that you are a slave to righteousness. In other words, obeying what is right before God is your new nature. It comes naturally to you, and there is no way you can act contrary to that. You are no longer under the tyrannical rule of the old nature of sin that caused you to live in fear, hate, and disobedience to God. You are now a slave to righteousness and are mandated to do what is right and acceptable to God:

Don't you know that when you offer yourselves to someone as obedient slaves, you are slaves of the one you obey — whether you are slaves to sin, which leads to death, or to obedience, which leads to righteousness? But thanks be to God that, though you used to be slaves to sin, you have come to obey from your heart the pattern of teaching that has now claimed your allegiance. You have been set free from sin and have become slaves to righteousness. (Romans 6:16-18 NIV)

When slavery is mentioned, many people get uncomfortable and rightly so because there is nothing good out of human slavery and the slavery imposed by the devil. Many who are under the bondage of sin can testify firsthand about how ruthless a taskmaster's sin is and how helpless they are under its tyranny. No matter how much they struggle to break free, the more difficult it gets, and the deeper they sink into their misery. Activities that start as pleasurable and fun have become tormenting and painful. It leaves them desiring more and more, but never getting any satisfaction. This type of slavery should be avoided by all at all costs. That is why the Bible admonishes us to flee from lust because it will destroy those it catches up with. In addition to slavery imposed by sin, humans have also subjected and still subject fellow humans to slavery. The consequences of this type of slavery have not been desirable, to say the least. There is nothing glamorous to belong to somebody else and to be owned and treated as property by another human being. The worst part is the fact that you lose your freedom and cannot come and go as you wish.

In contrast to the horrors of slavery under sin and to other humans is the blessedness of being a slave to righteousness. It is the freedom that comes from becoming a new creature in Christ Jesus and to break free from the yoke of sin and gain the ability to say no to the appeal of sin and walk in victory. You are no longer at the mercy of your feelings and the enticement of the flesh to fulfill its lust. Instead of darkness engulfing and destroying you, the light of God flows through you and illuminates your life and those that you come across. The death that accompanies sin is no longer associated with you because as salt, you bring flavor and preservation to a dying and decaying world. This implies that wherever you go and whoever you meet will benefit from this hope that you carry. Therefore, it is a good thing to be a slave to righteousness because it protects you from the present decay and death and rewards you now and forever with eternal life.

At this point, are you still wondering, "Why me?" There is something about you that makes you suitable to be used by God to make a difference not only in the lives of the immigrants but in the lives of all people that you come across. We have already touched the fact that you are light. Let these words of Jesus drive that fact home:

You are the light of the world. A town built on a hill cannot be hidden. Neither do people light a lamp and put it under a bowl. Instead, they put it on its stand, and it gives light to everyone in the house. In the same way, let your light shine before others, that they may see your good deeds and glorify your Father in heaven. (Matthew 5:14-16 NIV)

Jesus boldly declared that you *are* the light, not that you *may* be light.

You are the light, and people in darkness are going to benefit when you let that light shine because it will make a difference in their lives. You are told to let your light shine because that is why the light is needed in the first place. If there is no darkness, there is no need for a light. You already know that we are living in a world filled with darkness because the devil deceived Adam and Eve to disobey God. This single act of defiance against God's explicit instructions ushered in darkness, decay, and death on the earth. It caused spiritual death to humans. That is why the greatest need of our day is getting people out of this great darkness into God's marvelous light.

If you still doubt if you are the right person for the assignment, consider the fact that you were once walking in darkness and destined for damnation and eternal separation from God. Somebody reached out to you and shared the truth of the love of God with you, and your eyes were opened. You saw the light and turned away from it according to this scripture:

For you were once darkness, but now you are light in the Lord. Live as children of light (for the fruit of the light consists in all goodness, righteousness, and truth) and find out what pleases the Lord. Have nothing to do with the fruitless deeds of darkness, but rather expose them. It is shameful even to mention what the disobedient do in secret. (Ephesians 5:8-12)

You know what it means to walk in darkness and the hopelessness of not knowing who you are, why you are here, and where you are going. The good news is that you are no longer walking in darkness but in the light, and you have a blessed hope in the resurrection of Jesus Christ and the place He is preparing for all who have accepted Him as Lord and Savior. You know now that you are a child of God, loved unconditionally, and that you will spend eternity in the presence of the Lord. Your future home is heaven, and there, all your tears will be wiped away. There will be no more death, pain, and suffering.

How can you, who was once destined to die and have found life, keep it to yourself and not share with others? You are expected to expose the works of darkness and to not have anything to do with it. Why is it important that the works of darkness be exposed? Because these works are shameful, and those who are walking in darkness and under the bondage of sin need to be liberated.

For this to happen, the works of darkness that are holding them captive must be exposed. There is nothing better than the word of God. You are not being called to offer your own solutions, ideas, or philosophy. You are a messenger, and all you are charged to do is to faithfully deliver the message of your Master. When you do that, the owner and originator of the message will defend it and fulfill whatever promises are in the message. The burden of proof is not on you but on the owner of the message. We get into trouble when we assume the responsibility of trying to become the source of the message.

If you still don't get it, and the question "Why me?" is still lingering in your mind, take a look at the following scripture:

Be very careful, then, how you live — not as unwise but as wise, making the most of every opportunity, because the days are evil. Therefore, do not be foolish, but understand what the Lord's will is. (Ephesians 5:15-17)

The days we are living in are evil because good is being called evil and evil good by some people. Who could have known that a time would come when the unnatural marriage between men will be legalized and sanctioned? These days, some churches are even celebrating the unnatural marriage between two women. How is this type of abomination possible among the people of God? What has changed: we the people of the Scriptures? The answer is obvious: the Bible declares that Heaven and earth will pass away, but the word of God will last forever.

The word of God is not left up to our evil schemes and perversion. To say that these days are evil is not an understatement. Since the Supreme Court's decision in the 1973 Roe vs. Wade case legalizing the killing of babies in the womb, more than 61,000,000 American babies have been brutally murdered. Some of these children have been torn limb by limb out of the wombs of their mothers. The days are indeed evil because the womb, which is supposed to be the safest place for the baby, has become the place of death and destruction. If he escapes being killed in the womb, a mass shooter is waiting to gun him down at a concert or in school. How many mass shootings need to happen for us to wake up to the violence and senseless evil that some members of the society are inflicting on others?

Are you still doubting that the days are evil? All you need is to turn on your television and watch the evening news. You are bombarded evening after evening with the manifestation of evil in all shades. Mothers killing their babies, white-collar crimes, racism, hatred, drunkenness, drug abuse, suicides, robberies, shootouts between the police and gangs, etc.

Even though the Bible clearly states that God created them male and female, some people are challenging this basic understanding of who we are and how to identify ourselves. The new trend is that of gender fluidity: you can become whatever you feel you are. If you think or feel you are a man but were born a woman, you can declare yourself a woman; if you were born a man and feel that you are supposed to be a woman, you can change yourself into a woman. Some people are pushing for the eradication of "he" and "she" and advocating for a genderless society. You may be saying that this has nothing do with you because you do not support or condone such behavior, but the laws of the land are going to force you out of business or into a position to celebrate this lifestyle sooner or later.

Therefore, because the days are evil, we are admonished to be very careful about how we live. There is no time to waste. We must make the most of every opportunity. When the Bible says every opportunity, it means EVERY opportunity. Remember that the souls of people are extremely important to God, and this includes all those who have migrated and continue to migrate to the West. The color of their skin, creed, culture, and socio-economic status do not matter. The important thing is that God loves them as much as He loves you, and He has already invested a lot towards redeeming them. The will of God, which the verse above is talking about, is for all people to be saved. You are an important player in this, and now is the time for you to find your place and occupy it.

In case you are still asking, "Why me?" have you forgotten that you are a soldier of Christ? In the following verses, Paul was talking to Timothy and reminding him of who he truly was and calling upon him to imitate Paul:

Join with me in suffering, like a good soldier of Christ Jesus. No one serving as a soldier gets entangled in civilian affairs, but rather tries to please his commanding officer. (2 Timothy 2:1-4)

Paul considered himself a soldier of Christ; that is why he called Timothy a soldier as well and asked him to step up and not get entangled in civilian affairs. When you are a civilian, you eat, sleep, and do as you please. But a soldier follows the commands of the commander and is required to be fit for battle. This implies that the soldier may not eat as he pleases, sleep anytime, or drink without consideration. In short, the life of the soldier is not carefree. You are a soldier, and Jesus Christ Himself is your commander-in-chief, and you must obey Him. In case you still doubt if you are a soldier, take a close look at the following Bible verses:

Put on the full armor of God, so that you can take your stand against the devil's schemes. For our struggle is not against flesh and blood, but against the rulers, against the authorities, against the powers of this dark world and against the spiritual forces of evil in the heavenly realms. Therefore, put on the full armor of God, so that when the day of evil comes, you may be able to stand your ground, and after you have done everything, to stand. (Ephesians 6:11-13)

Paul was writing to the church in Ephesus, and he instructed the entire church to put on the whole armor of God because there is a spiritual battle being waged by the evil one against all who call upon the name of the Lord Jesus, including you and me. It is important to note that civilians do not put on armors; only soldiers do that. Are you driving an armored car? The answer is no because you are not in the army, but those in the UNITED STATES OF AMERICA army do. They know they are at war and need the armored car. You are at war and need to put on the armor of God because the evil day is not only coming; it is already here.

Now, you may be wondering what this war you are involved in is about. The fight for people's souls was declared in the garden of Eden when the devil succeeded in deceiving Adam and Eve to disobey God by eating the forbidden fruit. This defiant act by Adam was a bold declaration that they wanted to become like God and could do without God. Does this sound familiar? How many people do you know who has declared that God is dead, and there is no need for God? The atheist is 100 percent sure there is no God, and anybody who believes in God is not sophisticated and intellectually astute. The war to eradicate God from the public sphere is in full swing in the **UNITED STATES OF AMERICA**, and you cannot continue to be indifferent. When a president in the person of Barack Obama mocks and taunts some Americans for clinging to their guns and their religion, this should be taken seriously. Here is exactly how he said it: "And it's not surprising then that they get bitter, they cling to guns or religion or antipathy to people who aren't like them or anti-immigrant sentiment or anti-trade sentiment as a way to explain their frustrations." [1]

If you think that this assault against your religious beliefs is going to stop any time soon, you are kidding. Then-presidential candidate Hillary Clinton, while talking about the issue of abortion, made the following statement:

"Far too many women are denied access to reproductive healthcare and safe childbirth, and laws don't count for much if they're not enforced. And deep-seated cultural codes, religious beliefs, and structural biases have to be changed." [2]

It is amazing how words are used to conceal the evil of murdering unborn babies. Hillary Clinton is hiding behind women's reproductive health to advocate the unchecked killing of unborn babies. According to her, "deep-rooted religious beliefs" must change. In her thinking, those of us who believe that we are created in the image and likeness of God and that before we were born, God knew us are living in la-la-land. We must catch up with the times and discard these outdated beliefs in the sanctity of human life. In her world, the following scriptures are

---

[1] "Obama: 'They cling to guns or religion'," Christianity Today, April, 2008, http://www.christianitytoday.com/news/2008/april/obama-they-cling-to-guns-or-religion.html (accessed February 24, 2018).

[2] Joel Gehrke, "Hillary Clinton: 'Religious Beliefs Have to Be Changed' to Accommodate Abortion," National Review, April 24, 2015, https://www.nationalreview.com/2015/04/hillary-clinton-religious-beliefs-have-be-changed-accommodate-abortion-joel-gehrke/ (accessed February 24, 2018).

outdated and should be deleted from the Bible:

> *"Before I formed you in the womb, I knew you,*
> *before you were born, I set you apart;*
> *I appointed you as a prophet to the nations."* (Jer. 1:5 NIV)

> *For you created my inmost being;*
> *you knit me together in my mother's womb.*
> *I praise you because I am fearfully and wonderfully made;*
> *your works are wonderful, I know that full well.* (Ps. 139:13-14 NIV)

> *The Lord said to her,*

> *"Two nations are in your womb,*
> *and two peoples from within you will be separated;*
> *one people will be stronger than the other,*
> *and the older will serve the younger."*

> *When the time came for her to give birth, there were twin boys in her womb.* (Gen. 25:23-24 NIV)

> *Did not he who made me in the womb make them?*
> *Did not the same one form us both within our mothers?* (Job 31:15 NIV)

> *This is what the Lord says—*
> *he who made you, who formed you in the womb,*
> *and who will help you:*
> *Do not be afraid, Jacob, my servant,*
> *Jeshurun, whom I have chosen.* (Isa. 44:2 NIV)

> *And now the Lord says—*
> *he who formed me in the womb to be his servant*
> *to bring Jacob back to him*
> *and gather Israel to himself,*
> *for I am honored in the eyes of the Lord*
> *and my God has been my strength.* (Isa. 49:5 NIV)

When Elizabeth heard Mary's greeting, the baby leaped in her womb, and Elizabeth was filled with the Holy Spirit. In a loud voice, she exclaimed: "Blessed are you among women, and blessed is the child you will bear! But why am I so favored, that the mother of my Lord should come to me? As soon as the sound of your greeting reached my ears, the baby in my womb leaped for joy. Blessed is she who has believed that the Lord would fulfill his promises to her!" (Luke 1:41-45 NIV)

This is not an exclusive list of scriptures that deal with the subject of the womb and the role that God plays in what happens in the womb. Just like the lie that the devil told Adam and Eve that they could become God if they ate the forbidden fruit, women are being told today that it is their body and their right to do whatever they want with it. This message is completely opposite and against the message that God is saying concerning how we are supposed to conduct ourselves regarding the sanctity of human life. The so-called women's reproductive right to murder her unborn baby is not a right at all. This is evil and must be called out and denounced. We are either following God or doing our own thing. Nobody is saying that the decisions that women have to make are not difficult, but the call to carry our cross and follow Jesus is a tough call, and God knows that we have what it takes to do it.

According to Hillary Clinton, we must give up our deep-seated Christian beliefs concerning this matter and adopt her own so-called progressive, modernized, or enlightened position. What is progressive about killing unborn children? What is enlightened about ripping a baby limb by limb and yanking it out of the womb? The sad thing is that Hillary Clinton, who wants us to abandon our "old" and outdated ways, believes that a baby, no matter how old, can be killed as long as it is still in the womb. Why? During an interview on *CBS Face the Nation*, she was asked by moderator John Dickerson the following question, "Do you support a federal limit on abortion at any stage of pregnancy?"

She responded, "I think that the kind of late-term abortions that take place is because of medical necessity and, therefore, I would hate to see the government interfering with that decision. This gets back to whether you respect a woman's right to choose or not, and I think that's what this whole argument is about."[3]

---

[3] Steven Ertelt, "Hillary Clinton Supports Unlimited Abortions Up to Birth, No

What? The whole argument is not about the sanctity of human life, but about the right of a woman to kill her own baby? Why does she not talk about the trauma these women go through after giving permission for their children to be killed? Has she forgotten the guilt these women have to put up with for the rest of their lives? It is sad that a person holding such a view almost became the president of the UNITED STATES OF AMERICA. She had an interview in 2015. In 2016, when she was running for president, she was asked again in a debate if abortion should be restricted in late pregnancy, and she repeated her position that there should be zero tolerance, even if the baby is nine-months-old in the womb.

The following question was posed to Hillary Clinton by Chris Wallace, the moderator of the debate. "Secretary Clinton, I want to explore how far you believe the right to abortion goes. You have been quoted as saying that the fetus has no constitutional rights, and you also voted against a ban over late-term, partial-birth abortion. Why?"

"I do not think the United States government should be stepping in," Clinton said in defense of the partial-birth abortion procedure. "Because Roe v. Wade very clearly sets out that there can be regulations on abortion so long as the life and health of the mother are taken into account. And when I voted as a senator, I did not think that that was the case. The kinds of cases that fall at the end of pregnancy are often the most heartbreaking, painful decisions for families to make.

I have met with women who have, toward the end of their pregnancy, get the worst news one could get that their health is in jeopardy if they continue to carry to term or that something terrible has happened or just been discovered about the pregnancy, I do not think the United States government should be stepping in and making those most personal of decisions. So, you can regulate if you are doing so with the life and health of the mother taken into account."[4]

Limits Even in the 9th Month," Life News, September 21, 2015, http://www.lifenews.com/2015/09/21/hillary-clinton-supports-unlimited-abortions-up-to-birth-no-limits-even-in-the-9th-month/ (accessed February 25, 2018).

[4] Steven Ertelt, "Hillary Clinton Defends Killing Babies in Partial-Birth Abortions:

This type of reasoning is part of the battle you are up against, and cannot pretend there is neutral ground. Some people have decided to compartmentalize their lives, and anything concerning the sanctity of human life is placed in the social issues compartment, and some label it a "grey area."

The danger of compartmentalization is that it is dangerously pervasive, and all areas of your life are going to be affected. The issue of immigration that this book is addressing is one of those issues that may have been placed in a grey compartment. They do not see why something has to be done to engage all these individuals who have no business being in these countries. In their minds, whatever happens to these people is their fault because they were not supposed to move in the first place.

Those of us in the household of God cannot think like this. We know better not to let the world tell us how to be one another's keeper. We understand that the earth is the Lord's and all the people that are in it. Therefore, when God brings us in contact with people, no matter the context, we must deal with them as God will because we are God's people.

Let me reiterate here that I am not an advocate of open borders and illegal immigration. Lawlessness should always be discouraged, for, in the long run, it harms everybody because the outcome is anarchy, corruption, and failed societies. This should be a good enough reason for you to engage those that have moved to this country because if they are not reached in time and shown how to live here, they will repeat some of the undesirable customs that caused them to move in the first place. People do what they are used to doing because they like what is familiar, predictable, and comes naturally to them. Never forget that it is not enough for somebody to show up on the shores of the **UNITED STATES OF AMERICA**;

"Government Shouldn't Step In"," Life News, October 19, 2016, http://www. lifenews.com/2016/10/19/hillary-clinton-defends-killing-babies-in-partial-birth-abortions-government-shouldnt-step-in/ (accessed February 25, 2018).

they have to learn what it takes to get assimilated and become an integral part of the country.

If you are still not convinced that instead of asking "Why me?", you should be asking, "Why not me?", I want you to consider the fact that in addition to being a soldier of Jesus Christ, you are a priest of God Almighty. This is one of those areas that many denominations pay lip service to. They talk about the priesthood of every believer, but the way they are set up contradicts this core aspect of our faith.

In most circles, the pastor is the only "official" priest, and the rest of the congregation is considered to be lay and not in the ministry. The "real" ministers are the apostles, prophets, evangelists, pastors, and teachers. Some have even taken this order to mean that the gifts are ranked in order of importance, with the apostle being the highest-ranked and the teacher the least. No wonder you hear of an apostle so-and-so, prophet X, evangelist Z, and pastor K, but you never hear of teacher anything. Nobody wants to have this lowly title because it is associated with the least of the gifts. This subject requires an entire book altogether, but, for now, let us focus on the fact that you are not in some part-time ministry, and you are not a layperson or an auxiliary of anybody's ministry. You are a priest of God and a minister of the Gospel. This, not something that you are claiming to be or trying to be, is who you are, and everything else about you must flow from this understanding. The call to the priesthood has already been made, and God himself has already ordained you to function as a priest based on the following scriptures:

As you come to him, the living Stone—rejected by humans but chosen by God and precious to him—you also, like living stones, are being built into a spiritual house to be a holy priesthood, offering spiritual sacrifices acceptable to God through Jesus Christ. (1 Pet. 2:4-5 NIV)

But you are a chosen people, a royal priesthood, a holy nation, God's special possession, that you may declare the praises of him who called you out of darkness into his wonderful light. (1 Pet. 2:9 NIV)

Once you were not a people, but now you are the people of God; once you had not received mercy, but now you have received mercy. (1 Pet. 2:10 NIV)

These Bible verses are not suggestions or figurative, as some have made us believe. God says we are ALL priests, and that is who we are.

Read the verses carefully and take note that the last part of verse 9 is talking about ALL of us being called out of darkness into the light of God. Nobody disputes this, nor do they say it is figurative. In verse 10, it is talking about the fact that those of us who were not God's people are now God's people. Again, nobody has any difficulty accepting that we are God's people. Why, then, do they have an issue with us being a chosen people and a royal priesthood? Why do we have the clergy-laity divide today? Where did this idea come from?

By now, you may be thinking that the true ministers are those that have been called into "full-time ministry," and for you to minister, you must be either an apostle, prophet, evangelist, pastor, or teacher. Wait a minute. Where did that come from? According to the following scripture, the work of the ministry is to be done by the saints:

And He Himself gave some to be apostles, some prophets, some evangelists, and some pastors and teachers, for the equipping of the saints for the work of ministry, for the edifying of the body of Christ, till we all come to the unity of the faith and of the knowledge of the Son of God, to a perfect man, to the measure of the stature of the fullness of Christ. (Eph. 4:11-13 NKJV)

Jesus gave these different gifts to do one thing and one thing alone: to equip the saints for the work of the ministry. This implies that the ministry is carried out by the saints after they have been equipped. Unfortunately, we have it backward these days. Many erroneously think that it is the sole responsibility of the pastor to do the work of the ministry. This type of thinking is not supported by scripture, and now is the time to walk away from it. All believers are already called into full-time ministry, for they are priests chosen and ordained by God Himself. For the body of Christ to be edified and for all believers to become matured, the people of God must follow the instructions God Himself has given. Failure to follow the blueprint will result in immature, weak, and dysfunctional followers of Jesus Christ who are vulnerable and will be deceived by strange doctrines.

At the beginning of this chapter, I asked a crucial question that I have tried to answer. The question was, "Why me?" I hope you agree that this is the wrong question to ask. Instead, ask, "Why not me?" You are here at a time like this because God has a special assignment for you. It will be a smart thing for you to get along with the program. God expects you to participate in advancing His kingdom, and all the immigrants that are pouring into the UNITED STATES OF AMERICA and many other western countries should be engaged with the good news of the Gospel. In addition to feeding, housing, and clothing these immigrants, the best thing that can be done for them is sharing the Gospel and leading those that accept the Gospel to have a personal relationship with Jesus Christ.

In the next chapter, we are going to dive deeper into why this is crucial.

Chapter 2:
The Need of the Hour

The influx of people into the UNITED STATES OF AMERICA and other Western democracies brings unique challenges and opportunities. This chapter is going to focus on the greatest need at the moment.

As an immigrant who moved to the UNITED STATES OF AMERICA more than fifteen years ago and recently became a citizen, this topic is dear to my heart because I know firsthand what it means to move to a different country and try to settle down and make a new life there. The day I landed on the shores of the UNITED STATES OF AMERICA, I had a single suitcase and did not have enough money to cover the cost of one semester in school. The little money I had on me was borrowed from money lenders in my country of birth at a whopping compounding rate of ten percent per month. I came in broke, in debt, and without any guarantees of scholarships or financial aid. Humanly speaking, my situation was dire, and I needed immediate help badly. But my situation was not as dire as it appeared because I was operating in God's economy and was on God's mission. God had instructed me to move to the UNITED STATES OF AMERICA for graduate school. I stepped out in faith, believing and trusting that God would take care of me. You can read the details of what transpired and how God took care of me in *Coming to America: A Journey of Faith*.

Many immigrants show up with little material possessions, and our immediate reaction is to feel that their greatest need is material. There is nothing wrong with taking care of people in need, especially strangers who show up on our doorsteps with nothing more than the shirts on their backs. This is a good place to start, and all should be done to meet the physical and material needs. There is nothing wrong with providing clothing, housing, jobs, etc. to all these people. Thank God for the generosity of the American people and for opening their country and receiving people from all over the world who are fleeing persecution, economic hardship, or looking for better educational opportunities.

Jesus himself taught us about the importance of meeting the physical needs of those in our midst that are in lack as recorded in the following verses in the book of Matthew:

"Then the King will say to those on his right, 'Come, you who are blessed by my Father; take your inheritance, the kingdom prepared for you since the creation of the world. (Matt. 25:34-40 NIV) For I was hungry, and you gave me something to eat, I was thirsty, and you gave me something to drink, I was a stranger, and you invited me in, I needed clothes, and you clothed me, I was sick and you looked after me, I was in prison and you came to visit me.'

"Then the righteous will answer him, 'Lord, when did we see you hungry and feed you, or thirsty and give you something to drink? When did we see you a stranger and invite you in, or needing clothes and clothe you? When did we see you sick or in prison and go to visit you?'

"The King will reply, 'Truly I tell you, whatever you did for one of the least of these brothers and sisters of mine, you did for me.'" Matthew 25:34-40

The king in this passage is referring to Jesus Christ Himself, and He was talking about what will happen when He returns to judge both the living and the dead. There is no way we can love God and not love people. When we love people, it will be demonstrated by what we do for them. This is not rocket science. We live in self-deceit when we claim we love all people but do not make an effort to care for them. Jesus did not end at rewarding those who care enough for other people to cloth, feed, and house them; He issued a warning to those who do not care because they will be punished:

"Then he will say to those on his left, 'Depart from me, you who are cursed, into the eternal fire prepared for the devil and his angels. For I was hungry, and you gave me nothing to eat, I was thirsty, and you gave me nothing to drink, I was a stranger, and you did not invite me in, I needed clothes, and you did not clothe me, I was sick and in prison, and you did not look after me.'

"They also will answer, 'Lord, when did we see you hungry or thirsty or a stranger or needing clothes or sick or in prison, and did not help you?'

"He will reply, 'Truly I tell you, whatever you did not do for one of the least of these, you did not do for me.'

"Then they will go away to eternal punishment, but the righteous to eternal life." (Matt. 25:41-46 NIV)

In the passage above, Jesus Christ, our Lord, and Master, did not sugarcoat His words. If we fail to take care of the strangers, feed the hungry, and give drink to the thirsty, then we are going to be punished eternally. Therefore, we cannot neglect this important responsibility of meeting the material needs of others, but we should not stop there.

Beyond these physical needs is a serious need that must be met if these people are to do well in the UNITED STATES OF AMERICA and eternally. Physical needs are temporal and will, sooner or later, not matter any longer. Failure to take care of their spiritual needs will have both physical and eternal consequences.

In so much as many people think that we are living in the post-modern age and spiritual things no longer count, we, the people of God, understand the perils of living under the bondage of sin and under the dominion of the devil. There is nothing more terrible than being spiritually dead. No amount of hunger, poverty, suppression, oppression, and suffering can compare to the pain and misery of living under the yoke of sin and spending an eternity separated from God. Therefore, there is no substitute for bringing the good news of the Gospel to all people in all places all the time. We cannot allow the pressures of our daily lives and the lure of what other people are doing to prevent us from meeting the most essential and crucial needs of the people that are pouring into our country.

There are only two categories of people that land on the shores of the UNITED STATES OF AMERICA: those who are saved and those who are lost. It does not matter what country they originate from, their level of education, sophistication, riches, or poverty. What really matters is their spiritual condition. If they have not accepted Jesus Christ as their Lord and Savior or been reconciled with God, they are not going to spend eternity with Him. The condition of their soul should be our paramount concern because we have found the source of life and are partakers of that life. Therefore, we should be able to pass it to others.

Later in the book, we are going to take a closer look at how to reach and connect with these two groups of people. How to engage those who are not yet reconciled with God is very different from how to engage those who are believers in Christ Jesus. Let us never forget that thousands of missionaries were sent out from the West to share the good news of Jesus with the rest of the world. It was like casting our bread upon the waters, and now, the bread is returning to us. There is a divine reason why God is not only sending people who need the Gospel, but also people who know the Gospel and our fellow brothers and sisters in Christ. Both will be used by God to bless America and the other countries they move to.

I fall into the category of those that heard and believed the Gospel before moving to the United States of America. I gave my life to Christ when I was 12-years-old, a second-generation Christian. My parents became Christians when they were adults. The German missionary couple who brought the Gospel to Cameroon was still there when I left the country more than fifteen years ago. When I arrived in the United States of America, my heart was saddened by some of what I witnessed and encountered. The image of Christianity that we had seen on television in Africa was completely opposite from the reality on the ground. I was expecting the Gospel to be mainstream but was shocked to hear that the Ten Commandments had been banned in public schools and public places. In addition to banning the Bible, prayer was also outlawed. I wondered why a country would decide to do such a thing? I had literally prayed my way to this country, had witnessed many answers to prayer, and understood the power of prayer in our lives.

In Cameroon, my country of birth, we had no problem praying in our public schools and reading the Bible in public. In fact, it is very common to hear the Gospel being preached in public transportation buses. People are not bothered by those trying to share the Gospel with others. Open-air meetings are held all the time and everywhere to share the Gospel. There is a healthy debate about the different religious beliefs, and it does not seem to bother anybody. In public schools, there is a set time for moral instruction, during which students choose whatever class to attend. For example, students that are Muslims go one way, and the Christians go another. Then, the Christian students will separate based on their denominations. This arrangement works for everyone, and there is little conflict. I attended a Roman Catholic boarding school, and they were tolerant enough for a pastor to come to the school on Saturdays to take care of our spiritual needs. We were also allowed to go out on Sundays to fellowship in a Protestant church, then returned to school after the service.

To say I was shocked when I saw the hostility towards the Gospel is an understatement. There are "No Soliciting" signs on people's doors, making it difficult to knock and share the Gospel with them. On the university campus, most of the professors mocked and ridiculed Christianity and anything that had to do with faith. I could not wrap my head around it. Here I was, sitting in class and firmly convinced that it was God who had asked me to come to the UNITED STATES OF AMERICA to study and indeed God was taking care of me miraculously, yet I was surrounded by people who thought that if God existed, He must have died thousands of years ago.

I remember a professor who said, "If God answered prayer, how can He listen to all the millions of people that prayed at the same time? How will this 'God' know who is at least responding to them?" It seems this professor forgot that humans have launched satellites that are capable of providing GPS directions to millions of devices at the same time. This illustration is limited and cannot be used to explain our God, who is not of space, time, and matter. Before everything else, He was, is, and will always be.

Another thing that came up is the whole idea that believing in evolution was the acme of scientific thought. The schools in Cameroon teach evolution, but it is not a dogma. It seems we had forgotten that some of the greatest fathers of science lived in a time when the theory of evolution was not yet established. Did that make them less of a scientist?

I was also surprised by the rewriting of American history and the deliberate effort by some to minimize and disregard the Judeo-Christian roots of the country. It is not uncommon to hear people say that America is not a Christian country. Whatever this means, I do not know. Those who make such pronouncements are quick to preach tolerance and inclusivity, but what they actually mean is that all other religions are welcome, but Christianity should be shunned, lambasted, ridiculed, and eradicated from the public sphere. There is so much talk about the separation of the church and state. To some, this means that Christianity must not be mentioned in the public sphere. This point of view is completely different from what we were taught before I moved here.

We were taught that the pilgrims were Christians who were escaping religious persecution in Europe, where the state churches were not tolerant of any opposing views. Everybody was expected to be a member of the state church if they wanted to practice their faith. In England, for example, the Church of England was the state church, and the king was the head of that church. All other Christians were not looked upon favorably. This led to the migration of some of these Christians to the UNITED STATES OF AMERICA and established the first colonies. They sure came with their Bibles, and America owes a lot to the Protestant work ethic and the initial schools established by the Puritans to educate people so that they can read the Bible. Shockingly, a school like Harvard that was established to train pastors is one of the campuses where Christianity is relinquished to the background.

The foundation of the UNITED STATES OF AMERICA is being threatened by those who are deconstructing her history, way of life, and beliefs. This shift has challenges and poses some serious threats to national unity and cohesion in the future. Those who argue that immigrants should not be assimilated assume that there is no difference between America and the different countries these immigrants are coming from. This is turning a blind eye to the fact that if things were going well in their native countries, they would not have moved in the first place.

Unfortunately, in our quest to make everybody feel good, we have thrown the baby out with the bathwater. What is wrong in accepting that all countries are not the same? Why are we uncomfortable in accepting the fact that people move to other countries because those countries have a lot more to offer than their countries of birth? It seems these days, because of political correctness, asking these questions is considered by some to be racist, hateful, and bigoted. It is wrong and totally unacceptable to call anybody racist or hateful because they suggest that people move because their countries failed them, therefore, forcing them to move to other countries where they consider to be better. It is high time the good people in this country stand up and begin to confront such divisive, unfounded accusations that make no sense.

The truth is that people move because the country where they were born is not delivering whatever they consider is what will make their lives meaningful, enjoyable, and fulfilling. Each person is different — that is why some move and some don't. We should not allow political correctness to prevent us from having this dialogue. There is nothing wrong with moving. Migration has always been part of the human experience, and it is not going to change anytime soon. Some people will always move no matter what because what will give them a sense of fulfillment may be found on the other side of the world.

We, the people of God, have to use righteous judgment in assessing the present situation and see beyond the news headlines and political rhetoric. We know that all things work together for the good of those who love the Lord, and this includes the present situation that the country is facing. Whatever the devil meant for bad, God is going to turn it for the good of the country, if we align ourselves with His plan.

Those who thought the UNITED STATES OF AMERICA could be changed fundamentally through the influx of immigrants from the four corners of the earth will be disappointed when we reach these immigrants with the Gospel of our Lord Jesus Christ, and they become born-again children of God. This will dismantle their agenda because these immigrants that will convert to Christianity will understand immediately that their rights are from God and not the government. Therefore, they will not be beholden to the government because they will also learn that God is their source, not the government. It will get even better when they are disciplined and equipped to become disciple-makers themselves, a process through which they will come to the realization that their true kingdom is the kingdom of heaven and they are here as ambassadors of the Most High God, and their first responsibility is to be a priest of the Lord.

Now, you are seeing why the greatest need is that of sharing the Gospel with the immigrants and disciplining them. This will position these immigrants to have both physical and eternal impact on the UNITED STATES OF AMERICA and the entire world. If you have a personal relationship with Jesus Christ, you know firsthand what that relationship has done and continues to do in your life. And it is not difficult for you to wish that for other people. This is what the love of God that we have received does in our hearts. Just as God loves the world and gave, we, too, have that capacity to love and give because we are recipients of the same love of God. Not only that, but our bodies have become God's temple.

In light of all that is happening in the UNITED STATES OF AMERICA right now, those of us in the household of faith who know God and are walking with Him, cannot retreat because we know we have the solution that the country and the world needs. We have the cure to the malady that is plaguing all humans from diverse backgrounds. Since Adam and Eve disobeyed God and sinned in the garden of Eden, their sin unleashed unprecedented havoc, darkness, decay, and death that have plagued mankind for millennia. This one act of disobedience led to Adam and Eve dying spiritually. All who came after them are also dead spiritually because sin is in our spiritual DNA. That is why the bold declaration about the universality of sin must be taken seriously by all. The Bible clearly states:

For all have sinned and fall short of the glory of God. (Rom. 3:23 NKJV)

When the Bible says all have sinned, it means ALL, including the immigrants that are coming in and are members of other religions. No person has not sinned and in need of forgiveness and reconciliation to God. The need for people to be forgiven and set free from sin is urgent: *"For the wages of sin is death, but the gift of God is eternal life in Christ Jesus our Lord.* (Rom. 6:23 NKJV)"

There is a severe penalty for sin, and this has a physical and spiritual dimension. No adequate words can describe the type of life waiting for those who will be separated from God forever. Some have tried to dismiss the idea of hell, but this will not make the subject go away. Jesus Himself taught about the existence of hell and those who will be sent there. It is our responsibility to warn others about this terrible place and how to avoid going there in the first place.

Thank God for giving us the gift of life through our Lord Jesus Christ. This implies that a way has been made for anybody who wants to be set free from sin and be reconciled to God. This reconciliation takes place after the individual is quickened to become alive spiritually. This process is initiated by God because He loves all humans without reservation. It is written:

For God so loved the world that He gave His only begotten Son, that whoever believes in Him should not perish but have everlasting life. For God did not send His Son into the world to condemn the world, but that the world through Him might be saved. (John 3:16-17 NKJV)

But God demonstrates His own love toward us in that while we were still sinners, Christ died for us. Much more than having now been justified by His blood, we shall be saved from wrath through Him. For if when we were enemies we were reconciled to God through the death of His Son, much more, having been reconciled, we shall be saved by His life. (Rom. 5:8-10 NKJV)

This is the greatest news ever, and we should be excited to share this wonderful news with other people, including all the immigrants that land on our shores. As simplistic as this may sound, we who have been forgiven and reconciled with God know that sin is the root cause of all the problems that are plaguing the world today, and the solution is in Jesus Christ. We know from firsthand experience the blessedness of being forgiven and receiving the new life in Christ Jesus because He is the only person who is not only qualified but earned the right to solve our problem with sin. It is written:

For if by the one man's offense death reigned through the one, much more those who receive abundance of grace and of the gift of righteousness will reign in life through the One, Jesus Christ.) Therefore, as through one man's offense judgment came to all men, resulting in condemnation, even so through one Man's righteous act the free gift came to all men, resulting in justification of life. For as by one man's disobedience many were made sinners, so also by one Man's obedience, many will be made righteous. (Rom. 5:17-19 NKJV)

Adam, the first man, disobeyed God, and this led to death for all mankind. Then Jesus, the second "Adam," showed up and obeyed all God's law. His obedience has brought in forgiveness and eternal life. The great news is that this righteous act that He accomplished can become ours if we accept it. In fact, Jesus did what we are incapable of doing. That is why salvation is a free gift of God, and none of us can boast that we have done anything to merit it. We freely receive this gift and should freely share it with other people. As D.T. Niles once wisely said, "Christianity is one beggar telling another beggar where he found bread." [5]

The idea that we have found bread is not abstract. Jesus Christ, Himself said: *"I am the bread of life. He who comes to Me shall never hunger, and he who believes in Me shall never thirst."* (John 6:35 NKJV)

We have come to Jesus and are partakers of this life-giving bread that has given us eternal life, and it is our responsibility to share this information with other hungry people who are trying to feed their souls with junk food. We do not need to look far to see that this spiritual junk food is unhealthy. The diet is based on feelings, what is popular and cool. If it feels good and everybody is doing it, do it. You should never deny yourself anything, for there is only one life, and everything ends after you die, so make the most of this life by having as much pleasure as possible.

---

[5] "D.T. Niles quotes," Thinkexist.com, accessed March 7, 2018, http://thinkexist. com/quotes/d._t._niles/.

The consequences of such a worldview play before us each time we turn on the television, listen to the radio, or surf the Internet. The moral decay of our culture is reaching epic proportions because sin is having dominion over many people. Those in bondage claim that it is their right to do whatever they want to do, but the bitter truth is that if they want to stop sinning, they will fail. In fact, many have tried on many occasions but always return to their vomit because they are slaves to sin. Many people claim they are free, but nobody is free. All of us are slaves to something. You are either a slave to sin or a slave to righteousness. There is no middle ground and no neutrality.

We live in an age where everything is relative according to some people, but when it comes to whose slave you are, the law of relativity does not work here. This law has never worked, and no matter how much we wish it worked in this generation, it is not working. Jesus said: *Very truly I tell you, everyone who sins is a slave to sin. 35 Now a slave has no permanent place in the family, but a son belongs to it forever. So, if the Son sets you free, you will be free indeed.* (John 8:34-36 NIV)

Jesus was having a conversation with the Pharisees who were claiming to be free because, according to them, they were the descendants of Abraham. Jesus was making them understand that their actions were not reflecting those of their father, Abraham. For example, why were they trying to kill Jesus if they were Abraham's descendants? This is the question Jesus raised, and these religious leaders of His day could not answer Him. If they were truly the descendants of Abraham, they would have known that Abraham himself was awaiting the fulfillment of God's promise to bless all the nations of the world through his descendants. This promise was referring to the coming of the Messiah (Jesus Christ), who will be sent to liberate mankind from sin and reconcile them back to God. This is why Jesus told the teachers of the law that true freedom was from Him because when He sets somebody free, that is when that person will be truly free.

All those advocating for the freedom to kill their unborn children, smoke marijuana, commit adultery, lie, cheat, etc. think these will bring them joy and satisfaction. But after the high from drunkenness, the hangover that follows leaves the individual more miserable than the fleeting pleasure they had. The adrenaline rush from an extramarital affair or hookups leaves people with broken hearts, disappointments, and sexually transmitted diseases. All the women that have been lied to are sacrificing their children on the altar of convenience so that they can be "free" to climb the corporate ladder, pursue academic degrees, or any other thing that their heart desires. They were never warned of the lifetime guilt and health implications that accompany the procedure.

Some of these people caught in all these vices know that there is a better way. They long to be free to do what is right because they have tried unsuccessfully to fill the void in their hearts with all these things, and it is not working. When they are alone and sober, they cry for help, but it seems help is never going to come. Some resort to just ending it by committing suicide going to come to dash.

There is somebody that wrote about this predicament, and it is good to learn from him. Like many who have tried to break the challenges of sin over their lives and do what is good, the apostle Paul felt the same misery and agony of knowing what is good and desiring to do it but being unable to.

So, I find this law at work: Although I want to do good, evil is right there with me. For in my inner being I delight in God's law; but I see another law at work in me, waging war against the law of my mind and making me a prisoner of the law of sin at work within me. What a wretched man I am! Who will rescue me from this body that is subject to death? (Rom. 7:21-24 NIV)

Paul admitted that he was helpless and needed help. All who are without Jesus Christ are wretched and in dire need of a savior, even though many of them may consider themselves "good people." This is something that this generation is good at. Because of political correctness, we consider all humans inherently good. This is false because, according to Jesus Christ Himself, none is good.

A certain ruler asked him, "Good teacher, what must I do to inherit eternal life?"

"Why do you call me good?" Jesus answered. "No one is good — except God alone." (Luke 18:18-19 NIV)

This individual who asked Jesus Christ about the requirements to be saved is called the "rich young ruler" in some translations. He was an individual who kept all Ten Commandments, yet he did not feel that he was good enough to be saved. In fact, he was correct because when he came to Jesus and was asked to go and sell everything he had and give it away to the poor, he could not do it. He went away with a heavy heart.

The sin of idolatry is running amok these days, and many people are not even aware of the idols in their lives. Anything in your life that is more important than God is an idol. Let me put it this way: if you would rather disobey God than give up whatever you are either seeking or holding so dearly, that thing has become an idol. Jesus knew where this rich, young ruler's heart issue was and went straight to it. Jesus did not play the seeker-friendly Gospel presentation that we have adopted these days and are filling our pews with individuals that are not regenerated.

If somebody is still claiming that they are good enough to merit God's approval, let them take a closer look at the following scriptures: *"All of us have become like one who is unclean, and all our righteous acts are like filthy rags";* (Isa. 64:6 **NIV**)

The best we can come up with may be good in our eyes and that of other people, but when compared to God's standard, it is filthy and cannot and will never match up. Just like the rich, young ruler, many moral people are quick to say that they have not done anybody wrong and have not committed any gross sins. In their own eyes, they are perfect and need nothing. Sin is missing the mark, and it is rooted in our desire to do it without God and to be our own god. Many people have fallen into the deception that Adam and Eve fell into when the devil tricked them into believing that God was trying to keep something from them by preventing them from eating the forbidden fruit. The devil lied to them and said that after they ate the fruit, they were going to know good and evil. In other words, Adam and Evil would become gods, and there would be no need for God in their lives. They bought into this lie, and it brought corruption and death to the entire human race.

The symptoms of separation from God are what we call sins, which include hatred, adultery, sodomy, anger, bitterness, murder, drunkenness, idolatry, debauchery, falsehood, selfishness, fornication, etc. Therefore, if you are separated from God, you are a sinner and need God's forgiveness and restoration. There is none that is good except God. It should be proclaimed boldly without fear or shame because it is the truth.

Unfortunately, many people find it offensive when they are presented with this liberating truth about their sinfulness because they believe in their own goodness and can even point to some of the good works that they have done and continue to do. Good works are not enough, according to the following Bible verse:

And though I have the gift of prophecy, and understand all mysteries and all knowledge, and though I have all faith, so that I could remove mountains, but have not love, I am nothing. And though I bestow all my goods to feed the poor, and though I give my body to be burned but have not love, it profits me nothing. (1 Cor. 13:2-3 NKJV)

Can you imagine giving all you have to the poor and even allowing yourself to be killed, and still it is not good enough? Those who claim to be good should evaluate their lives in light of these powerful verses. The issue is that what we call "love" is usually driven by other motives, which may be to gain control, dominate, receive something in return, or make us feel better or superior to the recipients.

Below is the true definition of love, and I have yet to come across anybody that embodies this kind of love:

Love suffers long and is kind; love does not envy; love does not parade itself, is not puffed up; does not behave rudely, does not seek its own, is not provoked, thinks no evil; does not rejoice in iniquity, but rejoices in the truth; bears all things, believes all things, hopes all things, endures all things. (1 Cor. 13:4-7 NKJV)

Can you imagine what would happen to the murder rate, divorce, war, and other human-on-human crimes if this type of love was practiced by just a fraction of the world's population? The prisons will be empty, and the lawyers and judges will be out of work. Can your love measure up to this definition of love? There is nobody on the face of the earth that can love like this using their own strength because humans are not God.

The Greeks have six words for defining love: Agape, Philo, Eros, and Storge.[6] Agape love is God's love, and the Bible defines this kind of love to be God, according to the following scriptures:

---

[6] Roman Krznaric, "The Ancient Greeks' 6 Words for Love (And Why Knowing Them Can Change Your Life)," Yes! Magazine, December 27, 2013, accessed March 9, 2018, http://www.yesmagazine.org/happiness/the-ancient-greeks-6-words-for-love-and-why-knowing-them-can-change-your-life.

Beloved, let us love one another, for love is of God; and everyone who loves is born of God and knows God. He who does not love does not know God, for God is love. In this, the love of God was manifested toward us, that God has sent His only begotten Son into the world, that we might live through Him. In this is love, not that we loved God, but that He loved us and sent His Son to be the propitiation for our sins. Beloved, if God so loved us, we also ought to love one another. (1 John 4:7-11 NKJV)

God is love. No other definition can capture the type of love that is described in 1 Corinthians 13:4-7. In fact, the entire Chapter 13 of 1 Corinthians discusses this type of love, and it is humanly impossible to love like that. The love that is so popular today is Eros (romantic love) and Philautia (love of the self). That is why it is common to hear people say they love each other, and after some time, they divorce because of irreconcilable differences.

It makes one wonder where long-suffering, believing, and bearing all things have gone. The answer is that what people described as love was a mixture of romantic feelings and love for self. Love for self always wins when challenges show up. Therefore, anybody who wants to truly love needs God. Otherwise, you will be doing your own thing and will not have any eternal reward.

This is not to say that we cannot do or should stop doing good works. We place the cart in front of the horse when we focus on good works without, first of all, being reconciled to God. Salvation is not by good works — it is a free gift from God. Therefore, nobody can boast that they have done something that has made them qualified to be accepted by God. The following verses in the letter of Paul to the Ephesians must be taken seriously:

For it is by grace you have been saved, through faith—and this is not from yourselves, it is the gift of God— not by works, so that no one can boast. For we are God's handiwork, created in Christ Jesus to do good works, which God prepared in advance for us to do. (Eph. 2:8-10 NIV)

God's grace is available to everybody on earth, and all who ask for it will receive it. You do not need to do anything special or change who you are to qualify for God's grace. It has already been extended to you; all you need to do is to receive it. This is the greatest gift ever, and the people of God should be excited to share this gift with all who are willing to receive it.

Contrary to many other religions where there is a long list of things you have to do to receive salvation, there is no laundry list in Christianity. God has taken the first step, made provision for our sins to be forgiven, and has already extended His unmerited grace to all. The moment you realize that you are a sinner, repent of your sin, ask God to forgive you, and accept that He has forgiven you, the grace of God is yours.

It is after this has transpired that you can begin to do the good works that God has already prepared for you to do. These are works that will flow from the new person that you have become in Christ because the Holy Spirit of God comes to live in you. Now that you are a partaker of God's love, and since you are in union with God, the capacity to love (Agape) is given to you. You no longer do anything out of selfish ambition or to be boastful and arrogant. You become a vessel for the love of God to flow and heal the sick and broken world. This is the great mystery that has been revealed to us: Christ in us is the hope of glory. We cannot keep this liberation news to ourselves because God allowed us here for that purpose. Everything else that we do must flow out of this understanding.

This is why it is a strange idea for us to reach out to those that show up on our shores because there are only two types of people that come here: those that are saved and those that are not. We are going to get into greater detail about how to reach these two groups of people. That said, the greatest need is to share the Gospel of Jesus Christ with all who come to our shores. Nothing can take the place of this, and we should prioritize it above all else.

The next chapter will be looking at some of the obstacles that may come between us and this crucial assignment. Let us dive in.

Chapter 3:
Segregation is Alive and Well

If everything was going well and all of us are getting along without any difficulties, this book would not have been written. During my fifteen plus years in the United States of America, I have observed and witnessed a few things that need to be addressed from the perspective of an immigrant. The purpose of this is not to complain, blame, or bash anybody. I said this because all of us in the household of faith are a work-in-progress and in need of God's grace. None of us is above the other; all of us have sinned and have been freely forgiven by God. Therefore, we are expected to freely forgive and extend grace to others. This is easier said than done, and I am very aware of this. That said, if I do not speak up, God will raise somebody else to do so because the need is great and must be addressed one way or the other. Therefore, I better obey God and do what He is prompting me to do. Writing a book or books on immigration-related issues was far from my mind, but the Holy Spirit impressed in my heart to write about this subject and the three prior ones that have already been written.

When somebody heard that I was going to write four books to try and make some sense out of our present immigration challenges, he told me, "We do not have time to wait to read your books before taking action." According to this person, there is so much at stake, and there is no time to waste. Action must be taken now! I will not fault him for thinking and speaking like this. He is making a valid point about the need for us to engage these challenges, but his method of resolving it is what I do not agree with.

For me, all I am doing is obeying the promptings of the Holy Spirit to call on the people of God in the West, especially in the United States of America, to wake up for it is a new day as far as reaching out to immigrants is concerned. This call is urgent because the demographics of the type of immigrants that we are receiving are changing rapidly, and we cannot afford not to reach them with the Gospel and help them transition into American life and become part of the country. It is a big mistake to allow immigrants to their own devices just because we are afraid to get too close to them.

The immigrants I am referring to in this book are ALL immigrants from the four corners of the earth. Every person who arrives at the shores of the United States of America with the intention of living here permanently and eventually becoming a citizen falls under this category. No attempt will be made to segregate the immigrants on nationality, race, color, or religious affiliation. When people moved to the United States of America or any other country, they share a lot in common because they are being driven by almost the same needs and desires. The underlying commonality is the need for better opportunities and maybe escape from some sort of hardship.

Unfortunately, when these different people who are being pulled by the same desires and needs get to the United States of America, the conditions on the ground slowly start enabling them to become segregated into different groups. In the long run, the result of this segregation is a fragmental and "tribal" country that can lead to clashes and other hostilities. This is not written to scare you. If we continue on the trajectory of diversity, inclusivity, and sensitivity accommodation that has become so popular, we are setting the country up for a lot of problems in the future.

All this can be avoided if we reach out to immigrants as soon as they come in. You may be saying that a lot is being done in that regard. That is true to some extent, but more needs to be done because there is still a lot of segregation in the country.

Many words today have lost their meanings, and people have turned them into weapons. The word "segregation" is loaded with a lot of negativity and historical baggage, so I hesitated to use it here. There is no point in undermining the historical significance and impact of institutionalized and legally sanctioned segregation in the United States of America. Over the years, a lot has been written about this subject, some trying to justify it while others are condemning it.

Here, I will be pointing out the segregation that is inherent among all humans. This does not, in any means, downplay segregation that is set up to take advantage of other people, look down on them, or place them in a disadvantageous position. That said, it is important to understand that part of the result of the fall is the need for us to belong to a group and to keep others out of the group. This is usually not motivated by love, but by fear. We have not been given the spirit of fear, but of boldness and a sound mind. I would be spinning my wheels if I tried to have this discussion with those who are not spiritually-minded. I hope that most of those who will read this book understand spiritual things because the issues of segregation are a physical manifestation of a deep problem. We all know that the root of all human problems is sin. We know what the cure to sin is and how to take this cure to all who have been infected. The hope of the world, which includes the United States of America, is in our Lord Jesus Christ.

As has already been mentioned, segregation is something that humans like to do because we like to belong to a group that we are familiar with, share the same interests, beliefs, culture, etc. This is something that makes us comfortable because it is safe and predictable. There is nothing wrong with belonging to a group and being comfortable, but we cannot allow the need for comfort, familiarity, and predictability to become the main thing. Unfortunately, that is what is happening, perpetuated by the immigrants and enabled by those in the host countries. All this segregation is driven by the fear of getting out of our comfort zones and doing the things that do not come to us naturally. This excuse makes a lot of sense to us, but it will not make the cut when we look at what our Lord Jesus is calling us to do. We were never called to a life of comfort and predictability, but that of carrying our crosses and following Jesus Christ. More on this later.

Right now, you might say I am trying to make a mountain out of an anthill because segregation has been outlawed, and all of us are now free to mix and are, indeed, mixing. But this is just part of the story — the superficial part. You know well that morality cannot be legislated because the changes that need a change of heart must be accomplished by a change of heart. Desegregation is one of those changes that needs a heart transformation, not more laws. If the laws that are already written were doing the job, we would not be having this conversation. Unfortunately, our society is still segregated, although it is not the type of legalized segregation that America witnessed in the past. We still have a long way to go as far as the change of heart is concerned.

We are the people of the Book; we are the ones who know the truth, and we are the light. Therefore, we have to lead the way on this sensitive and divisive issue. If we do not, who else will? It is going to be challenging for some of us to accept that segregation is still alive and well and carries with it devastating, undesirable consequences for the country. No official policy says that immigrants should be allowed on their own to do their own thing, but when you look closely at how we are set up, especially in the body of Christ, you will realize that there is segregation that is going on. This is not a one-way street because it takes two parties for segregation to take place. This issue is perpetuated by the immigrants, and it is enabled, encouraged, and facilitated in some circles by the church in the West.

The following quote by Marin Luther King Jr. seems to be as valid today as it was when he made it on April 17, 1960. He said,

"I think it is one of the tragedies of our nation, one of the shameful tragedies at 11 o'clock on Sunday morning is one of the most segregated hours, if not the most segregated hours in Christian America. I definitely think that the Christian Church should be integrated and any church that stands integration and that has a segregated body is standing against the spirit and the teachings of Jesus Christ, and it fails to be a true witness, but this is something the church will have to do itself. I don't think church integration will come through the legal process."[7]

He made this statement before the 1964 Civil Rights Act that outlawed racial discrimination was passed. Before this law, racial discrimination had led to officially sanctioned segregation. Therefore, the Civil Rights Act was supposed to stop racism and, in so doing, deal a fatal blow on segregation. The church in the United States of America was operating under the laws of the country that had made discrimination based on skin color the right thing to do. It has always been difficult for me to come to terms with the fact that the church went along with the laws of the land instead of the law of God.

That said, this subject has not been brought up as an attempt to pass judgment or condemn anyone. It is a quest to understand where we have been, where we are now, and how we can move forward. There are a thousand-and-one directions this conversation can go, but it is warranted because there is a God way that is tied to Mission Dei that all who call the name of the Lord must adhere to. This is not an issue of whether if it is the right thing to obey God or not. Are we, as children of God, required to obey the laws of our country even when these laws contradict the clear teaching of the Scripture? When is it appropriate to stand up and disobey these laws that bring reproach to the name of our God? It is always appropriate to disobey any law, both the official law and unwritten social laws that are contrary to the Scripture.

During the segregation era, a few brave and courageous followers of Jesus Christ decided to stand with God and against the law of the land and the social norms of the day. Take the incidence that occurred in Chattanooga, Tennessee, in 1953, where Billy Graham did the unthinkable and held a desegregated crusade, even though the country was going through a time of violence resulting from racial

---

[7] Jason Tripp, "The Most Segregated Hour in America - Martin Luther King Jr." (video), April 17,1960, 0.52, https://www.youtube.com/watch?v=1q881g1L_d8 (accessed February 27, 2018).

tensions as a result of discrimination.[8] His action brought a lot of criticism from both sides, but he had made up his mind to do what was right and stood by it. If you think it was easy for him to do it, take a look at the following accusation that was leveled against him by a renowned theological professor at Union Theological Seminary, Reinhold Niebuhr, who felt that Billy Graham was somehow dumbing down the message of the Gospel and not making it complicated enough. Here is what Niebuhr wrote in a 1957 *Life Magazine* article:

Perhaps because these solutions are rather too simple at any age, but particularly so in a nuclear one with its great moral perplexities, such a message is not very convincing to anyone—Christian or not—who is aware of the continuing possibilities of good and evil in every advance of civilization, every discipline of culture, and every religious convention...[9]

The message that Billy Graham preached was about the love of God for all people and the need to respond to that love and accept God's forgiveness of our sins and extend that forgiveness to other people. That message has not changed; it was, is still, and will always be the solution that the world needs. We, who are in the household of God, have this solution and should not be afraid to share it with others because we are the only hope for a dying and lost world. We have made a lot of strides academically, scientifically, technologically, etc., but are still struggling with the basics of how to get along with each other.

Billy Graham understood this and took the lead. If the entire body of Christ followed his footsteps and did the right thing to do, maybe there would have been no need for the Civil Rights Act, and there would be less government intervention in our lives. Unfortunately, the people of God waited for the government to pass laws that "forced" them to do the

---

[8] The Christian Broadcasting Network, "Billy Graham Segregated Crusades - CBN. com," (video), 4:49, https://www.youtube.com/watch?time_continue=282&v=fsciF-Wj-REg (accessed March 2, 2018).

[9] Collin Hansen, "When Billy Graham Went to New York City," Christianity Today, 2005, http://www.christianitytoday.com/history/2008/august/one-last-gotham-visit-for-billy-graham.html (accessed March 2, 2018).

proper thing. This was a colossal failure because many in the household of God allowed fear to prevent them from standing up and challenging the status quo of their day. What if more people were bold and courageous enough? Perhaps, we would have had an entirely different outcome.

There is hope because we have examples like Billy Graham and people of faith in the Bible who stood up against ungodly laws and risked their lives to do so. They considered obeying God to be far more profitable than going with the flow and abiding by what was popular and sanctioned by the law of the land.

The case of Daniel, who ended up in the lion's den, is a strong testament to the type of exploits those who choose to obey God will do. A bad law was passed prohibiting prayer to any other, God and Daniel was not going to allow this law to prevent him from praying publicly. Remember that the purpose of this law was to get Daniel into trouble, and Daniel knew it, but he decided to stand his ground. Some will say that his actions invited the trouble that came upon him. Those that believe in self-preservation do not see any reason for Daniel opening his window for all to see him while he prayed. The "wise" thing for him would have been to close his window and go into his closet and pray. Over the years, some have wondered what point Daniel was trying to prove? Daniel understood something that all who complied with the law did not: he understood that it is better to please God and not man, and that his life was not his own but belonged to God. He also understood that we are not called to a life of comfort and self-preservation. He was not afraid of death because to die is to be with the Lord.

Let us go back to the issue of segregation and discuss why it is still persistent, especially among the people of God. This is such a nagging and complicated issue that needs an entire book to address it. But we should not shy away from talking about it because it is complicated. The issue is complicated because we have made it so. When the word of God gives us instructions about any subject, and we decide to do things our way, it gets complicated immediately. Therefore, the only way to reduce the complexity is to go back to the blueprint that God has laid down and follow it. God's view of the human race is as simple as a record in the following verses:

So, in Christ Jesus, you are all children of God through faith, for all of you who were baptized into Christ have clothed yourselves with Christ. There is neither Jew nor Gentile, neither slave nor free, nor is there male and female, for you are all one in Christ Jesus. If you belong to Christ, then you are Abraham's seed, and heirs according to the promise. (Gal. 3:26-29 NIV)

We are ALL one in Christ Jesus and should treat each other accordingly if we are the people of God. We are the people who are walking in the light and should be the ones to lead the way for everybody else to follow. Before modern science established that there is one human race, God Himself had already made it crystal clear. We are all one because we are all made in the image and likeness of God.

Unfortunately, some people think that they are superior to others and even use scripture to justify this twisted thinking. This type of thinking has persevered because there are those who have believed the lie that they are inferior, another twisted thinking that some have also justified with scriptures. How can anybody in their right mind declare that what God says is good is inferior? It is sad that some think part of the human race is cursed by Noah and are, therefore, subjected to a position of servitude forever. This is a lie from the pits of hell and must be confronted, exposed, condemned, and defeated. These so-called descendants of Ham that are cursed and so must remain cursed is a baseless concoction that needs to be called out and exposed for the fraud it is. Jesus broke all curses on the cross and has set all mankind free. Each time I hear preachers, both Black and white, talk about the Black race being a cursed race because they are descendants of Ham, it breaks my heart that we would rather believe lies than what God Himself has declared. Are all of us not the apple of God's eye? Did Jesus not die for all? Here is the prayer that Jesus prayed for His disciples shortly before leaving the earth:

I will no longer be in the world, but they are in the world, and I am coming to You. Holy Father, protect them by Your name, the name You gave Me, so that they may be one as We are one. (John 17:11 Berean Study Bible)

My prayer is not for them alone. I also pray for those who will believe in me through their message, that all of them may be one, Father, just as you are in me and I am in you. May they also be in us so that the world may believe that you have sent me. I have given them the glory that you gave me, that they may be one as we are one—I in them and you in me—so that they may be brought to complete unity. Then the world will know that you sent me and have loved them even as you have loved me. (John 17:20-23 NIV)

Before you jump to the conclusion that all the first disciples were Jews and therefore, living together and being one was not an issue, you should pay attention to the fact that if Jesus was praying for unity and oneness, it was because there was disunity among them. Secondly, Jesus also prayed for unity and oneness for all who will believe in Him through the ministry of the apostles.

All the people of God today are a direct result of the message that was preached by the early apostles, and we are expected to be one so that the world will know that we know God. Can it be that part of the reason our country and the world are having a hard time coming to faith in Christ is because we are so disunited? I am referring to all the people of God who are supposed to exemplify the unity that is found in Christ to a world that is clueless about what it means to be one.

There is no other verse in scripture that speaks so powerfully and succinctly about our oneness in Christ than the following verse in Paul's first letter to the brethren in Corinth: *"For we were all baptized by one Spirit to form one body—whether Jews or Gentiles, slave or free—and we were all given the one Spirit to drink".* (1 Cor. 12:13 NIV)

We are one body, and to think otherwise is to refuse the very scriptures that led us to a saving relationship with Jesus Christ, our Lord. There is no way any part of the body can claim to be more superior to others or feel that they are inferior and not worthy of belonging to that body. All parts of the body are there for a purpose; for the body to function properly, every part must do its function. Some parts of the body may not appear to make any sense to us, but no part of the body is useless, as modern science is discovering.

The appendix was one of those body parts that, in old biology books, was considered a vestigial part; in other words, useless that we can do without. Unfortunately, there was a misconception based on limited knowledge at that time. A recent study by Parker revealed that the appendix is a storehouse for much-needed bacteria in the body that can be released to replenish lost bacteria after a person suffers from diarrhea.[10] This implies that new knowledge about the appendix has shed light, illuminated our understanding, and cleared away the ignorance that clouded our judgment. The result is that our attitude towards the appendix is changing, and there are calls for more studies to be carried out to deepen that understanding. Doctors are now less inclined to readily cut out the appendix, as was the practice in the past. Instead, research is being done to figure out how to prevent the appendix from becoming infected in the first place.

This is just one example among thousands of others that can be brought up to illustrate how ignorance can lead to bad decision-making and bad attitudes. Therefore, it is imperative for us to communicate more and truly get to know each other before drawing any conclusions.

We have already mentioned that the root cause of segregation is sin, and it is manifested through fear and ignorance. The cure to this malaise is to gain more knowledge about other human beings. We, the people of the Book, do not need to go far to find out what the blueprint of humans is. We already have the Scriptures, God's own words, telling us exactly who we are and how we must conduct ourselves. In this case, we cannot continue to segregate ourselves from other people.

We started this chapter with the quote that Martin Luther King, Jr. made on April 17, 1960. Around 11 o'clock on Sunday morning was the most segregated hour. Is this still the case? What has changed, and what still needs to be done? These questions open a can of worms, with a thousand-and-one directions that we can follow. Please hold your peace and let us reason together and make an individual evaluation of where you are as an individual. There will be no attempt to make broad generalizations here because one size does not fit all.

People are at different stages of what I consider a spectrum of accommodation. On this spectrum are those who still hold that some people are superior to others; therefore, mixing on Sunday mornings or

---

[10] Charles Choi, "The Appendix: Useful and in Fact Promising," Live Science, August 24, 2009, https://www.livescience.com/10571-appendix-fact-promising.html (accessed March 2, 2018).

at any other time to worship does not make sense at all. Their solution to this is that the different "races" should meet separately and do their thing. The idea of people of all colors coming together to worship God (who created them) makes some people extremely uncomfortable.

There are those who think that it is the right and proper thing to do by making sure that each person worships God based on their traditions, culture, and history. They feel that it will be destructive to impose a particular style and way of worship on other people, especially immigrants who are coming from different backgrounds and have yet to understand "the American way." Those who advocate this say they are doing it out of love and concern for these immigrants who will be bored to death if they were forced to sit and listen to American preachers who are clueless about their culture, language, and where they are coming from. The best thing to do is to support these groups of immigrants to hold their own services in their languages, sing their songs, and do "church" the way they did in the countries they originated from.

There are a thousand-and-one reasons that have been and still are being given to justify why there are predominantly Black churches, Asian churches, Latin American churches, etc. But none of these reasons makes sense when the word of God and the bigger picture is taken into consideration. At the heart of all, this is fear and our desire to be comfortable. After all, in our seeker-friendly mindset, it is all about making sure that people who show up at church are comfortable because they are there for us to render them a service. When did the meeting of brethren to be equipped for the work of the ministry become a service that is offered to people who are expected to show up, pay, and be entertained?

We were never called to a life of comfort. I can already hear those who have contemporary and traditional services justifying why each group must be catered to based on their needs. Is it that we have come up with our own ideas of what the gathering of believers is all about? While the world around us is perishing, we are fighting over what songs to sing, how loud the band should or should not be. Wars are declared over the color of the carpet and the amount of lighting in the building. We can justify this segregation all we want and come up with a thousand-

and-one reasons to clear our consciences, but this will not make it right. The world is watching for the church to lead the way and show them what it means to walk in love, but the church is busy separating people into different groups because it is going to take too much for us to figure out how to get along.

Before you shoot the messenger, bear in mind that immigrant people of God are also guilty. There are Cameroonian, Ivorian, Congolese, Ethiopian, Bulgarian, Russian, Indian, Korean, Chinese, Filipino, Hispanic, Nigerian churches, etc. in the United States of America. Maybe this is the same situation in Europe and other countries where immigrants have moved from different parts of the world.

The situation gets even trickier because the Nigerian churches in some of the cities in the United States of America are also divided along ethnic lines. As such, it is not strange to find Yoruba churches and Ibo churches where the Yoruba and Ibo languages dominate the worship experience. How can you blame people who "enjoy" worshipping God in their own language, within their cultural context and experiences? Did God himself not make all these languages?

The quality of the answer you get is directly proportional to the question that you ask. You better be asking the right question if you expect to get an answer that will be of any good to you. The question should be, "Why did God leave me here on earth after I became a believer?" and for those that have migrated to different countries, "Why did God move me to a different country?"

It has never been for our comfort and will never be. We are having such a hard time getting along with each other because we are doing our own thing, and God has not been placed in the center. We may claim God is, but our actions are giving us away. How can you love God and hate people that God has made, just because they do not look like you? If this is not hypocrisy of the highest caliber, what is it? Who are we kidding? By their fruits, you shall know them. The world is sick and tired of us claiming to know the way, yet we are speaking and acting in ways that contradicted the instructions in the Manual that has been given to us to conduct our affairs. Your opinion has not been asked, so stick to the Manual. To claim that the Bible is too difficult to understand, that everybody has their own interpretation, or that there are too many different translations will not vindicate you from the responsibility of obeying the word of God.

It is a complex web, and the solution appears to be complicated, as well. If we simplify the situation, we will find out that the solution is much simpler than we think. The complexity is driven by fear — our need to be comfortable and our desire to experience the familiar and predictable. This is something that all of us are guilty of. There is nothing wrong with being comfortable or experiencing familiar things and having a predictable outlook, but when we allow our need for comfort to trump God's mission, then we are out-of-step with God and must repent and get back on track. The people of God, both the immigrants and those that are already in the land, have to repent and get right with God.

There is so much talk about preserving different cultures around the world and for people to experience God within their cultural settings. This is all well and good, but when this becomes an obstacle to the spreading of the Gospel and hampering the fellowship and unity that is supposed to be among the people of God, something is terribly wrong and must be corrected. We do not need to look far for a solution. Let the following words by the apostle Paul help us understand what we are called to do. He prioritized sharing the Gospel and winning others for Christ above everything else, including his comfort and cultural heritage.

For though I am free from all men, I have made myself a servant to all, that I might win the more; and to the Jews I became as a Jew, that I might win Jews; to those who are under the law, as under the law, that I might win those who are under the law; to those who are without law, as without law (not being without law toward God, but under law toward Christ), that I might win those who are without law; to the weak I became as weak, that I might win the weak. I have become all things to all men, that I might, by all means, save some. (1 Cor. 9:19-22 NKJV)

Where did we get the idea of turning the fellowship of the people of God into an exclusive country club? What I mean here is the idea that we make "our" church become exclusive and tailored to a particular group of people. At times, time segregation is done unintentionally, but in other cases, it is planned and implemented. There is no point insisting that people like to interact and associate with those that are like them and will be uncomfortable to mix with others that are different from them. This human reasoning makes sense to us, but it is contrary to the plan of God for reaching out and making disciples of all the nations and is hampering the spreading of the Gospel.

Based on what Paul is instructing us, we have to do all to win as many people as possible. This may mean sacrificing the style of music and traditions of "how" church is done. In the context of the present influx of immigrants that do not speak like us, eat like us, dance, and worship like us, we have to sacrifice to reach them. I am not suggesting that we commit any sin or disobey the laws of God to accommodate people. What I am saying is what Paul said: he made himself a servant that he may win many people. He became a Jew when it was necessary, a Gentile when duty called and even became weak just to win others for Christ. This should be our attitude towards those that do not know the Lord Jesus Christ and are brought in our midst.

The immigrants that are Christians MUST also understand why God took them out of their countries of birth to a different country. On the surface, it may appear as though they moved for better education or a better life, but at the heart of it, God moved them to use them to advance His kingdom. The immigrant Christians have to engage as well and resist the temptation of making their own thing because they, too, are uncomfortable and afraid of interacting with other people. God did not bring you to the United States of America to be a British, Nigerian, Russian, Bulgarian, Cameroonian, Italian, Nigerien, Romanian, Mexican, Australian, Cuban, etc. in America. God brought you to the United States of America or any other country that you may find yourself now to be used by Him to advance His kingdom. Whatever country you find yourself in needs you at this particular time – that is why God brought you there.

Unfortunately, the immigrants are guilty of segregating themselves because they want to maintain the familiar that governed their lives in their countries of birth. There is nothing wrong with dressing, eating, speaking, dancing, and worshipping God the way you did in your country of birth. But if doing any of these things is driven by pleasure, comfort, and ease rather than the leadership of the Holy Spirit, you are putting the cart in front of the horse and will stumble. If God wanted you to maintain your lifestyle, He would not have asked you to move to a different country.

Now that you have moved, it is time to grow up and adjust to the new country and learn how to be relevant. To insist that it is a good thing for the body of Christ to be segregated because we do not want to be uncomfortable is WRONG, plain and simple. This segregation under the pretext of cultural sensitivity is hampering the move of God in our time and dimming the light of God that is in us. How can we tell the world that we are all one in Christ, yet we cannot fellowship together? How can we tell the world that God created all of us, yet some of us think that others are inferior?

This is not a blanket statement, and I want you who are reading this right now to search your own heart and answer these questions. How do you view other people that are different from you? Do you think that some people are superior to others? Are you making any personal effort to diversify your friends and those that you are close to? Does it trouble you that the church you attend is made up of only people that look like you? Do you think that the right thing to do for other people is for them to hold their own services in their own language and cultural setting?

Right now, you may be wondering where all these questions are leading. You are right to wonder because some of the questions should not be asked. When you visit a church, and it has separate services along racial lines, and the reason given is that people need to be comfortable, you wonder what is going on. You have Hispanic services where those from Latin America congregate, African services for those from Africa, etc.

Some of the reasons for this division are pragmatic. For example, some of the people that have moved to the United States of America do not know how to speak English, and it will be difficult for them to sing the songs and listen to the message and communicate with the other members of the congregation. This reason is not strong enough to encourage these immigrants to set up their separate churches. How are they going to learn how to become integrated into American society or any other country they may find themselves in?

Meeting for fellowship is one of the most important ways through which people interact and get close to each other. Through this close interaction, values are transferred, and the support system helps to position everybody to do well. As people continue to interact, they get to know each other better, and racial barriers are broken because some of the fears that propagate these divisions are overcome. The result is that everybody benefits because the immigrants come in with some values that the host countries will benefit from. It can be as basic as learning to eat different types of foods that are healthier, and ways of handling conflict and relating to one another that is different from the American way. For example, in many other countries, people think mostly about the community; the American way is the individualistic way. This is good, but it has some drawbacks. Close interaction with other cultures will bring some necessary changes.

A pastor friend who leads a church for immigrants placed a new twist in the interpretation of the command that Jesus gave to the early apostles concerning how the Gospel has to spread from Jerusalem through Samaria and the ends of the earth. Jesus was wrapping up His stay on earth, and the apostles were asking Him about the events in the future and the timing of these events. According to this friend, Jerusalem was the people from his country of origin who are now living in a city in the United States of America where his church was located. The shocking thing is that this idea of reaching out to "his own people" was suggested by an American brother. This makes some sense, but it is part of the problem that is hampering the spreading of the Gospel and integration in the country. Such reasoning is out of context because when people move to a different country, they are not there to relive the experiences that caused them to be displaced in the first place. There is so much for them to learn in their new country that everything needs to be done to ensure that they are equipped with the necessary resources and tools that will make them successful in this new environment.

Where else should this start, but among the people of God who already have a lot in common? But just like the early apostles whose main preoccupation was restoring the kingdom of Israel and relieving them from the bondage imposed by the Romans, we want our immediate discomforts to be relieved. Unfortunately, this is not what God's intention is. If Jesus Christ Himself was not spared discomfort and suffering, why do we expect any less? What is so difficult in looking for ways to fellowship with other brothers and sisters in Christ? The answer may just be in the fact that, by default, we want to take care of us first. According to the following verses, their main concern was about the restoration of the kingdom of Israel:

Then they gathered around him and asked him, "Lord, are you at this time going to restore the kingdom to Israel?"

He said to them: "It is not for you to know the times or dates the Father has set by his own authority. But you will receive power when the Holy Spirit comes on you, and you will be my witnesses in Jerusalem, and in all Judea and Samaria, and to the ends of the earth." (Acts 1:6-8 NIV)

These early apostles still did not get it, even after spending three-and-a-half years with Jesus, listening to Him talk over and over about the kingdom of God and illustrating it with parable after parable. Even after Jesus died and rose from the dead, the apostles were still ethnocentrically driven by the desire for the kingdom of Israel to be restored. They could not process why God was allowing the Romans to occupy their country. It is surprising that on the cross, Jesus asked God to forgive those who were killing Him and did not call the legions of angels to come to His rescue and wipe out all these bad people. Jesus endured the humiliating and shameful death on the cross. Those closest to Him only cared for their momentary pain, disgrace, and discomfort to be alleviated. Why could they not see the tyranny of sin that the rest of the world was subjected to, and the need to free them as well? Why did they miss the fact that spiritual oppression and bondage has far more implications than physical bondage?

Jesus was not going to have any of it. That is why He reminded them of what was essential. The promise of the Holy Spirit was not for them to build their "own thing" — it was to empower them so that they can take the good news to the ends of the earth. They were expected to start in Jerusalem but ultimately had to move out and share it with ALL people. The power of the Holy Spirit was going to be given to them to get out of their comfort zone and take the Gospel to people who did not look like them, eat like them, and speak like them. It was the dawn of a new day, and God was no longer going to be exclusively for the Jews. Other people, including the heathen Gentiles, were also going to become the people of God. This type of message was strange to the early apostles because up to this point, God was for the Jews alone, and His presence was restricted to the temple in Jerusalem. Therefore, anybody who wanted to meet God had to come to Jerusalem. Why was Jesus telling them to take the Gospel to people away from Jerusalem? This did not make sense to them. This is why after the Holy Spirit came upon the early church on the day of Pentecost, they set up shop in Jerusalem, and not much was happening concerning going to Samaria and the ends of the earth. If the church was not persecuted and scattered, they would have continued to maintain their culturally relevant good times in Jerusalem and having a good time at the expense of the greater mission — that of taking the good news to other people and places. Thank God for the persecution that broke out and scattered them, according to the following account:

On that day a great persecution broke out against the church in Jerusalem, and all except the apostles were scattered throughout Judea and Samaria. Godly men buried Stephen and mourned deeply for him. But Saul began to destroy the church. Going from house to house, he dragged off both men and women and put them in prison. **Those who had been scattered preached the word wherever they went.** *Philip went down to a city in Samaria and proclaimed the Messiah there.* (Acts 8:1-5 NIV)

God's mission will be accomplished even if it means that persecution will be a vehicle that will be used to accomplish it. The price that God had paid to redeem mankind was too high, and He will do all to accomplish His mission no matter what. If we want Him to push us around to get out of our comfort zones and traditions, God will do it. The early church waited to be dragged into prison for them to get their act together. Some of them lost their lives because the instruction to go was not followed.

How are we doing regarding this command to reach all nations? The whole world is coming to us, and we are erecting walls and building stronger barriers to keep them out of our lives and our neighborhoods. We are turning our church buildings into exclusive country clubs where we meet on Sunday, listen to feel-good messages, and do nothing with them. We pride ourselves on walking in obedience because we show up to church every Sunday, listen to some good music, a nice message, and then go home. This checklist-Christianity will not bring about the radical transformation and establishment of the kingdom of God because it is tailored to take care of *me* and make *me* feel good.

Let us not get distracted from the task ahead and what we are actually trying to accomplish. Just because somebody shows up on the shores of the United States of America, he or she does not automatically become Americans. In other words, it is not enough for them to show up; they need to be equipped to live in this country so that they thrive and reach their full potential. When each person is equipped to function at maximum capacity, they will be more productive, and everybody will benefit. On the other hand, if we do not engage and give the necessary tools to these future Americans, their growth will be stunted, their productivity will be hampered, and all of us will suffer.

I can hear some already asking what this has to do with them because, in America, everybody pulls themselves by their bootstraps and makes things happen. There is some truth to this, but everything has to be taken within context. If not, we risk the temptation of throwing out the baby with the bathwater. Most immigrants are already highly motivated individuals and high achievers because it takes a certain caliber of people to pack and move to a different country to start all over. That is why in the United States of America, we look with pride at our ancestors who left Britain and moved to the new world to start afresh. The tales of all that they went through and their bravery are the subject of many novels and movies. We proudly recount and retell these acts of courage, bravery, and sacrifice. These stories of heroism do not end with those that landed on the east coast. We have also included those that pushed westward and opened the western front and eventually occupied an entire continent, connecting the east coast to the west coast to form what we know now as the continental United States of America.

A few years ago, I was driving down to Miami, Florida, with my family for a vacation. A sense of awe overwhelmed me as I meditated on how the earlier immigrants were able to occupy the entire continent. There was a sudden sense of wonder and appreciation of their bravery, tenacity, and vision. Maybe I felt like that because we have driven through more than 25 states and covered more than half of the country. My sense of marvel is not, in any way, diminishing the conflicts, wars, and deaths that occurred as a result of the occupation of this waste continent. Whenever history is told or written, some win and others lose.

I am not here to judge history, but as a person who believes in divine providence and knows that all things work together for the good of those who love God, I know that the events and the affairs of men do not take God unawares. God is still in control and will make use of the good, the bad, and the ugly if we hand them to Him.

We celebrate these heroes of the past but should not stop at them. Today, many other heroes are braving everything and showing up on our shores and will become the ancestors of the future. We who are already on the ground should treat them with this expectation, with the understanding that they have something to offer. If we partner with them, America will become stronger and better. We have to stop looking at them as a threat or a liability, but as huge potentials that can be tapped into. Many hardworking immigrants are doctors, lawyers, professors, accountants, nurses, janitors, drivers, etc. Their contribution to the growth and prosperity of the United States of America cannot be underestimated.

The call in this chapter for those of us on the ground who are people of the Book is to shift our focus and look at the bigger picture. First, eternity should be our ultimate goal, and we should be doing all to reach out to as many people as possible with the Gospel of our Lord Jesus Christ.

Second, we should focus on the future of the United States of America because the immigrants in our midst are going to become part of the country, and it is in our best interest and that of the country if everybody does well. When each person is bringing their A-game and is highly productive, the entire society and even the world will benefit.

Can the people of God start tearing the walls of segregation and lead the way for the rest of the country to follow? In the next chapters, we are going to zoom in on how to do this. It is going to take more than eating in the same restaurants, sharing the same hotels, bathrooms, schools, etc. There is going to be a fundamental change of heart towards each other that is rooted in the fact that we are all made in the image and likeness of God and that the color of somebody's skin does not define who they are. We have to look at ourselves and face our own fears, stereotypes, and prejudices. Nobody will do it for you. No law will change your heart. You need to ask God to give you the capacity to love all God's people. This is serious because our relationship with God starts and ends on how well we love. Just like Martin Luther King, Jr. said in his famous *I Have a Dream* speech on August 28, 1963, delivered on the steps of the Lincoln Memorial in Washington, DC, "I have a dream that my four little children will one day live in a nation where they will not be judged by the color of their skin, but by the content of their character."[11]

Many are stumbling on this simple call to not judge people by the color of the skin, not only in the United States of America but across the globe. In many places, people that have fair complexions are always considered to be more beautiful and given preferential treatment. But those of us who are in the body of Christ have the capacity and the ability to judge people by the content of their character and not the color of their skin. Jesus had healed a man on the Sabbath, and the teachers of the law were on His case, demanding why He did it. They even wanted to kill Him for doing good on the Sabbath. This was when Jesus made the following statement: *"Do not judge according to appearance, but judge with righteous judgment."* (John 7:24 NKJV)

---

[11] Martin Luther king Jr., "I Have a Dream" (video), August, 28, 1963, 5:16, https://www.youtube.com/watch?time_continue=95&v=3P_s3ChZlRY (accessed March 13, 2018).

Passing judgment based on appearances simply means that we let what is physical, what we see with our eyes, to determine how we think, react, and respond to situations and even people. For example, when we meet people that do not look like us, speak like us, and dress like us, we may be tempted to allow these physical attributes alone to inform how we treat them. If we hold the distorted view that when somebody looks different from us, it means they are inferior, we will treat them as such.

Righteous judgment, on the other hand, is letting the Spirit lead us. Our spirit is in union with the Spirit of Jesus Christ, and we have the mind of Christ and will act and react in a way that will be pleasing to God. There is no racism, prejudices, and inferiority/superiority complex as far as God is concerned. God's love is for all, and He expects us to love accordingly and to treat everybody with dignity and respect. Jesus Christ did not suffer and die only for people with some special complexion; He died for everybody. Therefore, everybody is special to God and should be treated as such.

In addition to the call to judge righteously, we are also prohibited from showing any preferential treatment based on perceived social status. Nobody puts this more bluntly than the apostle James. He said:

My brethren, do not hold the faith of our Lord Jesus Christ, the Lord of glory, with partiality. For if there should come into your assembly a man with gold rings, in fine apparel, and there should also come in a poor man in filthy clothes, and you pay attention to the one wearing the fine clothes and say to him, "You sit here in a good place," and say to the poor man, "You stand there," or, "Sit here at my footstool," have you not shown partiality among yourselves, and become judges with evil thoughts? James (James 2:1-4 NKJV)

He talks about judgment with evil thoughts. In other words, if we ascribe value to people based on their outward appearance, our judgment is tainted, and it is evil. There is no room for preferential treatment among the people of God. If giving preferential treatment based on the economic status of people is evil, how much is more using the color of somebody's skin to determine who they are and how we relate to them? We who are in the body of Christ know better and should lead the way for the rest of the world to follow, not the other way around.

We are called to love our neighbor and not just those that look like us. Jesus Christ used the parable of the good Samaritan to hammer this point home. For Jesus to suggest that a Samaritan was a neighbor to a Jew was revolutionary, to say the least. The Samaritans and the Jews did not associate with each other because the Jews considered them not to be worthy enough to be the people of God. Therefore, they had a disdain for them and even avoided passing through their cities when traveling from Judea to Galilee. The question I have for you is, are people with other skin complexions your neighbors? According to the Bible, the answer is YES! All people on earth are your neighbors, and you are commanded to love them according to the following verses:

If you really fulfill the royal law according to the Scripture, "You shall love your neighbor as yourself," you do well; but if you show partiality, you commit sin, and are convicted by the law as transgressors. (James 2:8-9 NKJV)

Showing partiality is evil and wrong, and the people of God should not go down this road because the result is always undesirable. Most of the racial tensions, hate, and segregation can be done away with if we can agree on the simple fact that we are all human, and none is superior to the other.

This idea of equality is rooted in Scripture and was not new, or something Martin Luther King, Jr. was inventing when he delivered his famous *I Have a Dream* speech. Even the founding fathers had the same understanding because they made the following declaration to that effect: "We hold these truths to be self-evident, that all men are created equal, that they are endowed by their Creator with certain unalienable Rights, that among these are Life, Liberty and the pursuit of Happiness."[12]

"All men" here is referring to all humans on earth because all are made by God with certain rights. How can we, in good conscience, call

---

[12]   *Civics and Citizenship Toolkit: A Collection of Educational Resources for Immigrants,* rev. ed. (Washington D.C.: UNITED STATES OF AMERICA Citizenship and Immigration Services, Institute of Museum and Library Services, UNITED STATES OF AMERICA Govt. Printing Office, 2007), 1.

that which God has declared good inferior? Is it possible to take away these God-given inalienable rights from other people? We can try to, but it will backfire and lead to a lot of social issues and turbulence. Therefore, it is in our best interest to ensure that we refrain from using the color of the skin to classify and categorize other people and let this inform how we relate and treat them.

It is unfortunate that we have to rely on the government to do something that is out of their jurisdiction. Our rights are not from the government; they are from God and God alone. We have to stop depending on the government to legislate our consciences and start allowing the Holy Spirit of God to lead us in doing what is good and acceptable before God. It is only when the body of Christ does this that our witness will have maximum impact and bring about the healing, hope, and restoration God intends to go through all of us. Now is the time to make ourselves available and to let the Holy Spirit move in us and through us to accomplish the will of our Heavenly Father.

I have demonstrated that allowing the need for comfort, predictability, security, and the familiar, though not wrong in itself, can lead to segregation, which can become a stumbling block to the Gospel. Also, segregation is not something that is restricted to the host country; immigrants also fall into the temptation of segregating themselves because of the challenges inherent to integration. They, too, want the familiar, secure, and predictable. It is important for the body of Christ to rise and fill the gap so that the kingdom of God can come, and healing can take place in the world.

In the next chapter, we are going to look at your role in bridging the gap and fulfilling Mission Dei in your generation. This book is geared towards the people of God in the West, and it is not referring to any race. If you migrated many years ago and have become a citizen of the United States of America, you fall into the category of those that are in the West; whether you agree or not, those that are coming in after you look at you differently because you have more experience and know the ropes better than them.

Chapter 4:
What Is My Role?

God needs you so He can accomplish His mission of redeeming and reconciling a lost world to Himself. You are part of the divine plan, and nobody can do what God has already planned for you to do. There are no spectators in God's army; ALL of us have been called to partner with God in Mission Dei. In this chapter, I am going to dive deeper into what Mission Dei is and your role in it.

First, I think it is important for me to reiterate why this book has been written in the first place. The purpose is not to point fingers and play the blame game. Such an attitude is ungodly and counterproductive. Each time you point one finger at somebody, four fingers are pointing back to you. Most of the time, what we are accusing others of reflects where we are. In the previous chapter, I discussed segregation at length and pointed out that everybody is involved in it. For it to stop, ALL of us must be willing to face our fears, doubts, misconceptions, stereotypes, and prejudices, for these things are found in all of us. The next step is for us to get out of our comfort zones and engage other people who do not look, speak, dress, and eat like us. This is a tough call, and it is going to require some dying to self and sacrifices for us to be successful. The good news is that we have what it takes to make this happen because we are the people of God, and His Holy Spirit is inside each of us.

This book is not meant to make anybody guilty. It is a call for the body of Christ to come together and be who they really are — the light and salt of the earth. Unfortunately, salt inside the salt shaker is of no good. Not until it gets out of the shaker and touches food, then the seasoning and preservative power of the salt is felt. In the same way, a light that is covered is useless because those in the dark will not be able to benefit from the light even though it is shining. If we are not careful, we can allow our saltiness and light to be blocked and prevented from fulfilling their purpose when we allow our fears, doubts, misconceptions, stereotypes, and prejudices to get in the way. All of us have the propensity to allow the familiar, predictable, and comfortable to prevent us from doing what is right. The desire is there, but the discomfort and pain that accompany change can hold us back, and we resort to giving excuses and justifying our unjustifiable positions. This is an extremely important issue. We should not take it lightly because Jesus Himself talked about the fact that salt can become useless:

"You are the salt of the earth; but if the salt loses its flavor, how shall it be seasoned? It is then good for nothing but to be thrown out and trampled underfoot by men.

"You are the light of the world. A city that is set on a hill cannot be hidden. Nor do they light a lamp and put it under a basket, but on a lampstand, and it gives light to all who are in the house. Let your light so shine before men, that they may see your good works and glorify your Father in heaven. (Matt. 5:13-16 NKJV)

The call to be light and salt is not a suggestion because we are already light, and we are expected to be who we are. Anything short of this is out of the norm, and it is an indication that we are not functioning the way we are supposed to. We are going to be focusing on how to be light and salt within the context of the influx of immigrants into our communities. While there are talks of building walls and deporting immigrants, the people of God have to adopt an approach that is in line with what God's Mission is. There is a place for walls and deportations, but the overall decline of Christianity in the West and the moral decadence that is becoming more and more prevalent was not caused by the immigrants.

The issue lies squarely at the feet of a church that grew rich, comfortable, and complacent to the one thing that they have been called to be. That is to be light and salt. We allowed our pursuit for material comforts and prosperity to get in the way of our being light and salt.

For example, at work, many of us are afraid that we are going to be fired if we let anybody know that we are followers of Jesus Christ, much less try to share our faith with those who are lost and dying around us. It is easy to talk about sports, the weather, fashion, and other things, but the Gospel is a no-no. We have allowed political correctness and the desire to fit in and be loved and accepted by all to stifle our testimony.

This is more than sad because we have the solution to all the darkness around us and the decay in our culture, but we are keeping it to ourselves. All of us will agree that if somebody found the cure to cancer and decided to hide it, that person would be considered wicked. It will be justifiable for him to lose his license, be locked up, and have his/her name eradicated from human history forever. Many of us will wonder why anybody in their right mind will do such a callous thing. While this is an example that makes some sense, it pales in comparison to what is happening right now to those who have not been reconciled to God through Jesus Christ and will spend an eternity without Him.

Sin is the spiritual cancer of our time, and the consequence is physical and spiritual death. If you have been forgiven and reconciled to God and your dead spirit quickened for you to become born again, you have firsthand experience of the benefits of becoming a child of God. You have been blessed with spending eternity in the presence of God, where there will be no more pain, sorrow, or death. How can you keep this cure to sin all to yourself and not share it with others? Is it because you do not believe you have the cure, or is it because you think the momentary pleasure being enjoyed by those under the bondage of sin is good enough for them? Are you afraid that these people will have momentary suffering because they have to start walking in righteousness? What about the promise that you are also holding up, which clearly says that:

For I consider that the sufferings of this present time are not worthy to be compared with the glory which shall be revealed in us. For the earnest expectation of the creation eagerly waits for the revealing of the sons of God. (Rom. 8:8-9 NKJV)

There is some amount of suffering that followers of Jesus Christ are going to endure, but it is nothing compared to the reward that is awaiting them. When you compare this suffering to the slavery and bondage of sin and the eternal separation from God, it is worth suffering in this life. Therefore, we should not allow the thought or fear that those that we present the Gospel to are going to go through some inconvenience prevent us from reaching out to them and sharing the greatest news ever. We, too, are going to suffer for the sake of the Gospel, and this should not stop us from identifying that we know Jesus.

As for your role in God's mission regarding the immigrants that He has brought into your community, it is important to understand why that role is pivotal and why it is crucial that you fulfill it. The Westminster Catechism asks this crucial question:

What is the chief end of man?

Here is the answer that is given, "Man's chief end is to glorify God, and to enjoy Him forever."[13]

There is nothing wrong with glorifying God and enjoying him throughout eternity. This is going to be the starting place for us to understand what God has in mind. The Westminster Catechism emphasizes the importance of the word of God revealed in both the Old and New Testaments and how crucial this word is in informing us how to glorify God and enjoy Him. In other words, there are no other instructions or directions for us to follow because the infallible word of God is sufficient. Their reliance on the word of God to inform us is to be commended because we live in a day when the word of God is being attacked left and right and discredited by man. But the word of God has not changed and will remain the same forever. Therefore, we can rely on the word of God to guide our conduct and inform us about our role.

To glorify God and enjoy Him forever, we must identify what He likes and develop a liking for it as well. How can we say that we are glorifying God, but have a disregard for the things that are dear

---

[13] Center for Reformed Theology and Apologetics, "WESTMINSTER SHORTER CATECHISM WITH PROOF TEXTS," Fisher's Catechism, www.reformed. org/documents/wsc/index.html?_top=http://www.reformed.org/documents/WSC. html.

to His heart? There is one thing that is closest and extremely dear to God's heart, and it meant so much to Him that He sacrificed His only begotten Son for it. If God were like us who sleep and get up each day, I would have said that when God gets up in the morning, the first thing that comes to His mind is people. But we know that He that watches over Israel never sleeps nor slumbers. God never sleeps, and it will be heresy to question that. The point being made here is that God loves people because they are extremely important to Him. This is not something that is made up. God has demonstrated this love through the sacrifice of His Son and the grace that He has extended to all. God loves us unconditionally and has made provision for the forgiveness of our sins. We, the people of God, are called to love just as our heavenly Father is love. We cannot claim we love God and hate the people that He loves.

Your role is to love these people that are coming in droves, even though they may not be lovable. You were not lovable when God extended His love to you. Now that you have benefited from the love of God, you have the capacity to love because God is living in the inside of you and is ready to use you if you are only corporate with Him.

The question is, what does it mean to love others? It is a legitimate question, and it is one that was asked more than two thousand years ago by a teacher of the law who was interested in knowing what the greatest commandment was. At the heart of this question was his desire to please and glorify God. We must be interested in knowing what we can do to glorify God and please Him. It is reported in the Gospel of Matthew that a teacher of the law came to Jesus and had the following conversation with Him:

But when the Pharisees heard that He had silenced the Sadducees, they gathered together. Then one of them, a lawyer, asked Him a question, testing Him, and saying, "Teacher, which is the great commandment in the law?"

Jesus said to him, "'You shall love the Lord your God with all your heart, with all your soul, and with all your mind.' This is the first and great commandment. And the second is like it: 'You shall love your neighbor as yourself.' On these two commandments hang all the Law and the Prophets." (Matt. 22:34-40 NKJV)

The Pharisee was trying to trick Jesus, but he forgot that Jesus did not only know the word — He was the word. Jesus did not get into some lengthy arguments with him on some doctrinal position. He referred to a verse in Deuteronomy that says, *"Hear, O Israel: The Lord our God, the Lord is one! You shall love the Lord your God with all your heart, with all your soul, and with all your strength."* (Deut. 6:4-5 NKJV)

It is crucial to understand that after quoting this verse, Jesus went ahead and included: love for our neighbors. If you look at this verse superficially, you may think that Jesus was adding a new command. This is not the case because Jesus said that, *"On these two commandments hang all the Law and the Prophets." (Matt. 22:40 NKJV)*

He was saying that if you love God and love your neighbors, you have obeyed both the New and Old Testaments. How could Jesus condense the entire 66 books of the Bible into one commandment of LOVE? Jesus could do this because love is not a feeling or driven by emotions. Remember, we already described what agape is (unconditional love or divine love). This is love that is demonstrated and never expects anything in return. It is a love that flows from God Himself. Therefore, when we get reconciled to God, the capacity to love is given to us. We can now walk in the love of God and show that same love to others.

Now, let us take a close look at the reason Jesus was able to reduce the entire Bible to love. If you look at the Ten Commandments, the first four deal with our relationship with God, and the remaining six are about our relationship with each other. This implies that if you love God, you will not have any other gods beside God, you will not make yourself a carved image and bow down to it, you will not take His name in vain.

In the same light, if you love your neighbor, you will not murder them, commit adultery with their wife or husband, steal from them, bear false witness, and you will not covet their house, wife, servants, ox, car, nor anything that belongs to them.

Now, you see why Jesus made it clear to the Pharisees that all the commandments are summed up in love. Our interaction with others is motivated by love, God's love, that we have freely received, and are required and expected to share with others. Your role is to love God, and to love God requires you to spend time with Him and get to know

Him better. When we love anybody, we spend time with them, talk with them, and listen to them talk to us as well. There is no way a relationship will grow without investing time in the relationship. One way to spend time with God and talk to Him is through prayer.

Do not be anxious about anything, but in every situation, by prayer and petition, with thanksgiving, present your requests to God. And the peace of God, which transcends all understanding, will guard your hearts and your minds in Christ Jesus. (Phil. 4:6-7 NIV)

Here, we are presented with a simple yet powerful way to pray. Having gratitude and thankfulness for all God has already done and has promised to do for us is the best place to start. It is only after we have expressed our gratitude to God that we can ask God for the things that we need. A heart of gratitude will bring us peace that is beyond all human understanding; those around us will marvel at our resilience in the face of difficulties and hardship.

The other part of our relationship with God is Him speaking to us. The word of God is the one infallible way that He speaks to us, and through it, we know who He is, what He likes, dislikes, and expects from us. No wonder the Psalmist says: *"Your word I have hidden in my heart, That I might not sin against You".* (Ps. 119:11 NKJV)

To walk in obedience to God, we must hide His word in our hearts, and the sure way to do it is to ensure that we read the word of God daily and meditate upon it. We must make a conscious decision to read and study His word. There is an excellent Bible verse in which God emphasizes the need to know His word:

This Book of the Law shall not depart from your mouth, but you shall meditate in it day and night, that you may observe to do according to all that is written in it. For then you will make your way prosperous, and then you will have good success. (Josh. 1:8 NKJV)

Reading, studying, and memorizing the word of God gives something for us to meditate upon. The more we meditate on the word of God, the stronger our faith will be, and the more victorious our walk with God is going to be.

Nobody exemplifies this better than our Lord Jesus Christ. When He was tempted by the devil, He used the word of God to defeat the devil. He did not attempt to reason, argue, or convince the devil. There was not even an attempt to interject His own opinion. All He did was use the word of God, and this kept the devil at bay.

If the word of God was good enough for Jesus, it should be more than good enough for us. Unfortunately, many people like to interject their own opinions when they are confronted with temptations. It is not uncommon to hear people say, "Left to me, according to me, in my opinion, I think a good God will not send anybody to hell or not allow same-sex individuals who 'love' each other to get married." Who asked for your opinion, and what makes you think that how you feel is more important than what the word of God is teaching?

The word of God is the same yesterday, today, and forever and it never grows old or out of fashion. "Thou shall not kill" has not changed, and we all know that it is a wrong thing to kill. All this is being said to underscore the importance of God's word and the need for us to allow it to lead and guide us. If immediately you say, "According to me, God is not so-and-so," then you are in danger of making your own god in your own likeness. To avoid falling into this idolatry, you should refrain from letting your own opinion lead you. Allow the word of God to take the lead, not the other way around.

As has already been pointed out, people are extremely important to God. The entire Bible is actually God's divine plan to redeem mankind. After Adam and Eve disobeyed God in the garden of Eden by eating the forbidden fruit, God went to work immediately and set a plan of redeeming, reconciling, and restoring mankind back to where they were before the terrible fall.

God immediately promised that He was going to send the son born of a woman that was going to crush the head of the devil. This was the promise of sending Jesus Christ, who was going to smash the head of the devil, defeat sin, and set mankind free from the bondage and the consequences of sin. After this promise, God called Abraham and promised him that all the nations of the world were going to be blessed through him. This was reaffirming the promise of sending Jesus Christ through whom all the nations of the world will be blessed and are being blessed as we speak. Eventually, Jesus Christ was born of the Virgin

Mary after being conceived through the power of the Holy Spirit and was crucified on a Roman cross, betrayed and condemned by His own people. Though the devil conspired to kill Jesus Christ and eventually landed the fatal blow, unfortunately for him, God had the last say. Here is what actually happened:

In Him, you were also circumcised with the circumcision made without hands, by putting off the body of the sins of the flesh, by the circumcision of Christ, buried with Him in baptism, in which you also were raised with Him through faith in the working of God, who raised Him from the dead. And you, being dead in your trespasses and the uncircumcision of your flesh, He has made alive together with Him, having forgiven you all trespasses, having wiped out the handwriting of requirements that was against us, which was contrary to us. And He has taken it out of the way, having nailed it to the cross. Having disarmed principalities and powers, He made a public spectacle of them, triumphing over them in it. (Col. 2:11-15 NKJV)

What appeared to be a defeat in the eyes of a casual observer was actually a fatal blow to the devil and the power of sin. Jesus totally disarmed the devil, principalities, powers, and spiritual forces in high places. In addition to defeating and disarming them, all the ordinances they had against us were also destroyed. This is why we have true freedom in Christ Jesus because He purchased it on the cross with His blood, and now, we can partake of it free of charge. We can also invite other people to come to Jesus so that they can be freed by Him.

So far, we have seen that loving God requires that we pray and study His word. This is the first part of the great commandment. When you obey this part, you are going to obey the second part as well, not out of compulsion, but in response to God's love for you. As you spend time in God's word, it will be revealed to you how much God loves people, and you will, by default, love people as well.

This takes us to the second part of the great commandment, that of loving your neighbor as yourself. Many people wonder who their neighbor is. Jesus understood this and told the parable of the Good Samaritan, a well-known parable that has blessed many people over the years. Jesus told this parable because a Pharisee came to Him and tried to trick Him about who one's neighbor is. Maybe this was a follow-up to the fact that when Jesus answered the question about the great commandment, instead of just saying the first part that spoke about loving God, He added the second part of loving your neighbor as yourself.

The definition of neighbor that Jesus gave did not fit the one held by the Pharisees. In their minds, a neighbor was somebody that lived close to you and was of the same race, religious background and had the same culture and belief system. This distorted definition of a neighbor was used by the Pharisee to discriminate against the sinners, tax collectors, publicans, Samaritans, and Gentiles. The Pharisees were not allowed to sit with these people or even eat with them. This is why they had a hard time accepting that Jesus was the Son of God because He ate and drank with all these people that the Pharisees considered outcasts.

In the parable of the Good Samaritan, a man is robbed and left to die on the road between Jericho and Jerusalem. As the man was lying there fighting for his life, a priest on his way to the temple passed by and saw him but decided to keep going and did nothing to help the man or send anybody to help out. According to the priest, God was in the temple, and it was more important to "serve God" in the temple than take care of a fellow human who was in distress and in danger of dying. Then, a Levite passed by and did nothing as well. Jesus used these two religious leaders to emphasize the fact that we can be religious all we want but can still miss out on where God is and what He does and what He requires us to do.

Then, a Samaritan showed up and did not allow the fear of what might happen to him to prevent him from helping the man that was in need. The Good Samaritan cleaned the man's wounds, applied oil and dressed them, placed the man on his donkey, and walked to the next inn. Can you imagine how inconvenient this must have been for the Samaritan, be walking on foot while somebody is riding on his donkey? It is recorded that when the Good Samaritan took the man to the inn, he paid for him to be catered for. He asked the innkeeper to take care of the man until he recovered, and any extra cost was going to be billed to him, and he was going to come back and pay the bills. This was like giving an open check to the innkeeper.

Why would a Samaritan, of all people, show this type of reckless and boundless love? Samaritans were not considered to be the people of God, and nobody expected them to be up to any good. Some have even postulated that the Jews hated the Samaritans so much that even though the shortest route between Galilee and Jerusalem was to go through Samaria, many Jews avoided going through Samaria because they did not want themselves to become unclean by associating with Samaritans.

After Jesus finished sharing the parable, He asked the Pharisee who had asked about who his neighbor was, who he thought was a neighbor to the man who fell among thieves: the priest, Levite, or the Samaritan? The answer was obvious to the Pharisee, and there was no way for him to wiggle out of it.

So, which of these three do you think was neighbor to him who fell among the thieves?"

And he said, "He who showed mercy on him."

Then Jesus said to him, "Go and do likewise." (Luke 10:36-37 NKJV)

It is worth noting that the definition of your neighbor was expanded by Jesus beyond what was culturally expected, and the purpose was to ensure that we do not allow our cultural heritage to prevent us from reaching out to others. Jesus was saying that we are all neighbors and should not discriminate based upon skin color, economic status, or national heritage. The teacher of the law was not expecting this answer and must have been disappointed when Jesus told him, "Go and do likewise." This teacher of the law was being told that anybody that he finds in need has to be taken care of, irrespective of who they are or what the society thinks about them. Showing love practically has to take precedence over our conveniences, stereotypes, comforts, and preferences.

This was not a suggestion, but a command that did not just end with the teacher of the law; it applies to all of us today. We are all charged to go and do likewise. The priest and Levite, who failed to help the man who was robbed, beaten, and left to die, had very good reasons for not helping out. One of them might have been someone this man had robbed because he, too, had robbed others, and it was payback time. It could have been the fear of being attacked if they stopped to help — the man may be pretending, and the whole thing was set up to lure them into a trap. They might have also reasoned that going to the temple to perform their priestly duties was more important than helping somebody that was a nobody. What if they had died and made it them unclean? You see, religion can make us miss where God is and what He is doing.

Whatever reason the priest and the Levite gave for not helping the man was not good enough, and Jesus made it crystal clear that they failed to be a good neighbor to the man that was robbed. Are you a good neighbor, or have you allowed fear, stereotypes, and prejudices to prevent you from being a good neighbor? Some of the stereotypes and prejudices are hidden behind justifications that make sense to us and others, but we cannot hide behind convenience, fear, and false humility to continue segregating ourselves from each other.

The need ahead of the body of Christ is huge, and we cannot afford to stand on the sidelines and pretend to ourselves that these immigrants should sort out their mess. Some of these people ran away from disastrous situations and are hurting badly, and their wounds need to be cleaned, dressed, and oiled. Somebody will have to pay for the bills while they recover. Above all, this cannot be done at arm's length; there is a need for proximity and getting to know people and treating them with respect and honor, not just a project.

Let the action of the Good Samaritan inform us on how to proceed. He got off his donkey and allowed the man to use it while he walked on foot. This was just for a season and for a short distance, but he did all within his power to ensure that the needs of this valuable man were met. Unfortunately, we have been taught to be so self-centered and to preserve our lives and dignity that it is extremely difficult to interact with other people in a way that will bring healing and restoration. We should never forget that the immigrants of today are going to become the Americans of tomorrow. Therefore, we should reach out to them and equip them with the tools that are necessary for them to be successful so that all of us can have a successful future.

While some may wish they were not here in the first place, we know that it is better to engage, empower and equip because they are here to stay and will eventually become part of the fabric of the country. Therefore, it is prudent for those of us who are already on the ground to be facilitators and empowerment agents because all of us will benefit in the long run.

The other not-so-desirable alternative is to do nothing, bury our heads in the sand, and pretend these people are not even here in the first place. When we do see them, we hope that they disappear, and we move on with our lives without any disturbance or inconvenience.

While waiting for this new problem to sort itself out, we complain, grumble and blame the immigrants for moving here. We ask out of frustration and disdain, "Why did they not remain in their own country? Why did they have to move here?" If you are truly interested in the answers to these questions, you will engage the immigrants with the best this country can offer because most of these immigrants are on a quest for freedom, equality, justice, and opportunities to be all they were created to be. It takes a certain caliber of people to want it bad enough to pack and leave their countries of birth and move somewhere else, without any guarantees for success, coupled with all the risks and uncertainties involved.

Some people feel that those who pack up and leave are sellouts and cowards because they should have stayed and resolved the problems in their countries of birth. This is something that we can debate all day, but the answer is far more complicated. It will be unfair to make a blanket judgment. First of all, some must move for their destinies to be made manifest. Therefore, it is not unnatural for humans to migrate; they have always migrated and will continue to migrate. Second, we are all different. Each one of us has a unique assignment, and it is important that we have the freedom to pursue that assignment wherever it may lead us. There is no point distinguishing between the internal and international movement of people because at the heart of this movement is the desire for change and improvement. When we start looking at the movement of people from this perspective, it will help us appreciate what is going on and how we relate to those that move into our communities.

If anybody dares to suggest that the immigrants who moved from Europe to the Americas were cowards for running away from Europe and not staying back to fight and fix their countries, they will be accused of committing sacrilege. Our history books are filled with the bravery, tenacity, exploits, and achievements of immigrants. In the same light, let us not forget that some of those that are arriving on our shores today have the same fire for expansion, bravery, tenacity, and exploits in their veins and will move this great country to the next level. Therefore, it is in our best interest to engage and complement each other.

We who are part of the body of Christ have to be motivated by love to engage the strangers in our midst. Based on Jesus Christ's definition of who our neighbor is, we know without a shadow of a doubt that everybody is our neighbor, no matter their race, religious background, or belief system. It even gets more critical when we are talking about people who are in need and in spiritual and physical danger. We cannot allow our traditions and preferences to prevent us from loving our neighbors as ourselves. What we wish for ourselves, we should wish for others. It is not possible to be a follower of Jesus Christ and be a racist at the same time. There is no compatibility between love and discrimination.

Your role is to love God and to love your neighbor. We have seen how to love God; now, let us take a look at how to love our neighbor. It means showing care and concern for them that must be accompanied by action. This action must be practical. It is not enough to say you love people, but do not do anything for them. Nothing says it better than the following verse in the book of James:

What does it profit, my brethren, if someone says he has faith but does not have works? Can faith save him? If a brother or sister is naked and destitute of daily food, and one of you says to them, "Depart in peace, be warmed and filled," but you do not give them the things which are needed for the body, what does it profit? Thus, also faith by itself, if it does not have works, is dead. (James 2:14-17 NKJV)

You may be wondering why the verse above is not specifically talking about love, but it is quoted here. We are called to walk by faith, and the physical evidence that we are walking by faith is in the works that follow out of that faith. When we love, we are going to do something to the people that we love, just as God loved us and gave us His Son, we are expected to give to those that we love. The command is not just to love only those that love us, but to love our neighbors.

People have two types of needs: physical and spiritual. The apostle

James was talking about meeting the physical needs of those that we loved when these verses were written. While it is important to take care of the physical needs of people, it is more important to prioritize taking care of their spiritual needs because eventually, it is the spirit that will last eternally. This is not undermining the importance of the physical, but just stating the fact here. The souls of people are eternal, and we have to bear that in mind.

We in the body of Christ who have been saved by the blood of Jesus should love people enough to tell them about the greatest news ever. This is not pushing our faith on others by trying to make people become something they were not created to be. It is a matter of life and death, for we know that all have sinned, and the wages of sin is death, and Jesus Christ is the only way to God.

Let us not get tied down with the idea that there is one God, and all roads lead to Him. This is not true. The truth is that there are many different gods and different roads lead to them. Therefore, there is no need to insist on having just one god. Jesus made a bold claim that we have to take Him by His word. The exclusivity that Jesus claimed is either true or false – there is no middle ground. Jesus died for what He believed in, and after three days, He rose from death and ascended to His Father. The only way to the Father is through Jesus Christ, no other person. This implies that if anybody wants to go to the God that Jesus is calling His Father, you must go through Him.

How is this position preventing other people from pursuing their own gods? At the heart of the matter is the fact that there are many gods, but they are not the same, and people can pick and choose which god to believe in. Whichever god you choose will determine the outcome of your life. We who are followers of Jesus Christ, the only person who died and resurrected, have found the truth and should share it with other people.

We should love our neighbors enough to share the greatest news ever with them. Some have called this evangelism, and I will not get bogged down by terminology. What is important is that we love people enough to let our light shine. When they ask us why we are different, we should not be ashamed or afraid to tell them that we believe in Jesus

Christ and that He has changed and transformed our lives. That we have found forgiveness of our sins and that we have become children of the highest God and will spend eternity with Him. This is not a call to propagate our denomination or push our own agenda; it is a call to point people to the saving power of the Gospel of our Lord and Savior Jesus Christ. When we love people, they will respond to our message because we are not treating them as a project, but as other humans that need respect and honor.

The other dimension is helping these people grow in their Christian faith if they accept the forgiveness that Jesus offers. Others have called this process discipleship. Again, I don't want us to get bogged down by terminology.

Obeying the great commandment will result in us automatically obeying the great commission. It is impossible to be living in obedience to the great commandment without obeying the great commission. The great commission is one of the last instructions our Lord Jesus Christ gave to us before leaving the earth. It must be taken seriously because this command is at the heart of the mission of God. It summarizes the reason why God sent Jesus Christ to come upon the earth to suffer and die on a rugged Roman cross. Jesus did not die for us to "have a church" or build our ministries. The death of Jesus Chris is at the heart of God's redemptive plan. We who have been called and saved by Him have to get on board with what God is already doing. No wonder when Jesus was about to leave the earth, He issued the following instructions:

And Jesus came and spoke to them, saying, "All authority has been given to Me in heaven and on earth. Go therefore and make disciples of all the nations, baptizing them in the name of the Father and of the Son and of the Holy Spirit, teaching them to observe all things that I have commanded you; and lo, I am with you always, even to the end of the age." Amen. (Matt. 28:18-20 NKJV)

Jesus Christ started by saying that He has all the authority. In other words, we should not be afraid because our mission is not an illegitimate one. It is Mission Dei, and the power of authority to carry out this important mission has been given to Jesus Christ, and He is charging us to go with this understanding. Therefore, when Jesus Christ told the early apostles to be endowed with the power of the Holy Spirit, the purpose was for them to be witnesses for Him, starting in Jerusalem, Samaria, and to the ends of the earth.

Are you filled with the Holy Spirit? If your answer is yes, where is your witness? Are you telling others about what God has done in your life? Nobody comes in contact with Jesus Christ and remains the same. Jesus Christ transforms all who have an encounter with Him, and all we are required to do is to report what we have witnessed. It is not about your own ideas, feelings, or desires; it is about what Jesus Christ has done in your life. How was your life before you met Jesus Christ? What changed after you met Jesus Christ? How is your life now? This is the witness you are called upon to do.

The woman at the well who met Jesus Christ went back to her village and reported to the whole village what had transpired between her and Jesus Christ. The entire village then came with her to meet Jesus Christ and hear Him. You may be saying that this woman had it easy because Jesus was there in person. It seems that you have forgotten that Jesus ends the command by saying that He is going to be with us always. The presence of Jesus Christ is with us at all times, and we can point other people to Him and to what He has done and is doing in our lives.

At the core of the great commission is the instruction to make disciples, not converts. Jesus understood that making disciples will lead to multiplication and, eventually, exponential growth. On the other hand, making converts will result in a snail-paced increase in the number of people that will be saved. Few people have been assigned to do the work, while the rest of us have been told that we are to support these experts who are on the frontlines through our money, time, and other resources. Doing the work of making disciples seems to be above our pay grade. Where did this idea come from? Why would God save us, and instead of taking us immediately to heaven, He keeps us here on earth? Why are we here? To get a good job, make some money, eat good food, and die? Heaven is, by far, above anything this world can ever give to us, and if God does not take us immediately to walk on the streets of gold and instead, allows us to stay on these dirty streets of the earth, there must be a big reason.

Maybe you were raised and taught that it is the responsibility of the "clergy" to make disciples while you, the "laity," play a supporting role. This thinking is in direct opposition to what the role of the apostles, prophet, evangelist, pastors, and teachers are supposed to be doing. The instruction is straightforward: equip the saints for the work of the ministry. It is more than being an usher, a greeter, a choir singer, or performer in the church drama club. All these things have their place, but what should be at the forefront is making disciples of all the nations, and this is something that ALL children of God are called to do. Every single one of us, not a select few, is expected to make disciples. You do not need to be an apostle, prophets, evangelist, pastor or teacher to make disciples. All you need to be is a born-again child of God that is filled with the Holy Spirit.

Unfortunately, the functional gifts that were given to the body of Christ to equip and empower the people of God to minister to a lost and dying world have been turned into positional roles, to the extent we have even ranked them and made some more important than others. No wonder some people are covering the top and most prestigious titles and paying lip service to the priesthood of every believer. That is why you hear of apostle John, prophet Daniel, evangelist Jack, pastor Martin, but never teacher Lucas. Since the role of the teacher is listed last on the gifts, many have relinquished it to the background, and nobody wants that to be the prefix of their name. By the way, in the New Testament, Paul, Peter, James, and the rest of the apostles never referred to themselves as Apostle Paul or Apostle Peter; they always addressed themselves as Paul, the apostle, Peter, the apostle. Can it be our love with titles and positions that have gotten in the way of the most important assignment that our Lord Jesus Christ has given to us? It is high time this model is changed if we want to reach our generation with the Gospel of our Lord Jesus Christ and turn our world upside down, as the apostles did in their time.

The instruction to go make disciples of all the nations is explicit because Jesus expected His disciples to teach others everything that He had instructed them. This included teaching the next converts and turning them into disciples who will, in turn, do likewise. In other words, every disciple of Jesus will eventually learn how to do everything that He commanded and will teach others to do the same.

Are you a disciple of Jesus Christ? Then it is your responsibility to obey the great commandment and carry out the great commission. It is only when you do this that you will be living a life of obedience to the great commander, our Lord Jesus Christ. Anything short of this is being religious and claiming that Jesus is Lord while you are the person in charge of your own life and doing your own thing.

This is the sad reality of many people who claim to be followers of Jesus Christ. They are so remotely removed from the life of obedience and have allowed fear to cripple their testimony. Many cannot dare make their colleagues at work know that they are followers of Jesus Christ because they want to fit in and do not want to rock the boat. Do you know what cost Jesus Christ His life? He rocked the boat, refused to fit in, and did not take an opinion poll to carry out the mission that His heavenly Father sent Him on. Jesus was also not afraid of what people thought and said about Him. Do you know that He was called all sorts of names because He did not hang out with the right crowd? Here is what Jesus Christ said about himself:

"For John came neither eating nor drinking, and they say, 'He has a demon.' The Son of Man came eating and drinking, and they say, 'Look, a glutton and a winebibber, a friend of tax collectors and sinners!' But wisdom is justified by her children." (Matt. 11:18-19 NKJV)

Then all the tax collectors and the sinners drew near to Him to hear Him. And the Pharisees and scribes complained, saying, "This Man receives sinners and eats with them." (Luke 15:1-2 NKJV)

Each time you feel like name-calling is going to stop you from identifying with Jesus Christ, you should remember that He was called a "glutton, winebibber and a friend of sinners" because He refused to look down on those that needed Him the most. You are a disciple of Jesus Christ, and your motto should be, "I will do what Jesus will do in every situation!" You cannot allow those around you to define the agenda for you. Let Christ in you, the hope of glory, lead you. You may be saying that it is challenging and costly to stick your neck out for Jesus Christ. You are correct! It will cost you something, and if you refuse to identify with Jesus Christ in this life, He will shun you in the next.

The purpose of this book is to position you so that when you meet your Creator, you will be welcomed home with "Well done, thou good and faithful servant," not "Depart from me, you worker of iniquity. I know you not!" There is a great reward that is being prepared for those who will participate in Mission Dei. My prayer for you is that you take this mission seriously enough to play your own part. This is not placing some sort of burden on you. If you love God, you will want to please Him and do only things that will make God happy. God loves people, and you should, too, if you want to please God. Love people enough to share the good news of salvation with them. Love people enough to care about their souls and where they will spend eternity. It is not the sole responsibility of the pastor or elder to make disciples of all the nations; it is your responsibility, and you should not delegate it to others. It is easy to say, "I pay my tithe and give an offering to those that have been called to do the work." You must go beyond tithing and giving an offering. If you have been taught that this is enough, then you are majoring in the minor things at the expense of the more important ones.

Making disciples of every nation is the responsibility of ALL people of God. This includes you who have been born again and cleansed by the blood of Jesus Christ. You were not saved to give 10% to God and do whatever you want with the 90%. God demands 100%, and it is to your best interest if you are 100% in. The world is sick and tired of 10% Christianity. No wonder many Christians will rather take their 10% to church than reach out and help others who are in need because their motivation is for God to open the windows of heaven and pour down His blessings on them.

Like the priest and the Levite, we turn a blind eye to those who have fallen by the wayside because we want to participate in some religious function. The world does not need more religious people. The world needs people who are willing to be the light and salt — authentic followers of Jesus Christ whose lives align with their actions, and they love enough to share the reason for the hope that they have in Christ Jesus. This is your opportunity to take this challenge and run with it and become an authentic follower of Jesus Christ.

Part of our challenge is that we are doing our own thing and not what God commanded us to do. We are trying to "build the church" instead of "making disciples." There is nowhere in the Scripture that we are commanded to build the church. Here is what Jesus said: *"And I also say to you that you are Peter, and on this rock, I will build My church, and the gates of Hades shall not prevail against it".* (Matt. 16:18 NKJV)

The task of building the church is solely in the hands of Jesus and Him alone. Maybe part of the burnout among pastors and other church leaders is because they are busy doing something that they are not called nor equipped to do. The responsibility of making disciples is what the body of Christ has been charged with. After the disciples are made, Jesus Christ uses them to build His body, the church. It is time for a change, of course, and for the people of God to go back to the basics and do what they have been commanded to do: to make disciples.

For this important task to be accomplished and for Mission Dei to be carried out, you have to take your position and play your part. This is to love God and love your neighbor as yourself. This is not complicated, and in the next chapter, I am going to give you some practical ways that you can do this, especially with regard to the immigrant population. We have exciting days ahead of us because we know that whenever the devil means something for bad, God has a way of turning it for our good. Now is the time to position yourself and partner with God in accomplishing this crucial mission.

Chapter 5:
How Do I Participate?

We are running out of time to engage the immigrants that have flocked and continue to flock into our country. While the politicians are bickering back and forth about what to do with this crisis, pondering if all the illegal immigrants should be deported or given amnesty and erect a wall at our southern borders, the people of God have an urgent assignment to fulfill. Whatever decision the politicians make, our attitude towards both the legal and illegal immigrant population should not change.

We are people who love God and love our neighbors as ourselves. We know that all people, no matter their race, creed, and immigration status, are our neighbors. We must love them and love them enough to tell them the truth about their separation from God and the unconditional love that God has for them. We must love them enough to tell them that the United States of America is not heaven because, in heaven, there is no more death, no more sorrow, no more pain, and no more mass shootings.

Unfortunately, the United States of America, in her greatness and power, still has a lot of issues that need to be resolved. People still hate, murder, steal, segregate, lie, cheat, blackmail, and shoot each other. In other words, sin is still alive and well in the country, and the results are seen and felt on a daily basis.

We should love all people enough to let them know that our stay here on earth is temporary and no matter how good life in the United States of America is compared to other parts of the world, there is an expiration date on how long all of us will live on this earth. We should love people enough to tell those who are illegal, those who have willfully broken American immigration laws or the laws of any other country, that it is wrong to break laws because lawlessness harms everybody. We cannot be afraid to call people to order under the pretext of justice and love. What are we going to tell those that pay the price to obey the laws and do what is right? How is this fair to them? Let us love enough to challenge people to develop the moral character to do what is right because people of character and moral rectitude benefit themselves and the rest of society in the long run.

We cannot allow the fear of being called names to prevent us from practicing tough love. Here, tough love is referring to the courage to tell those who are breaking the law that it is wrong, ungodly, and counterproductive. If you think the immigration laws in your country are bad and harmful to all who want to move to your country, it is your responsibility to lead a massive protest for those laws to be changed. This is your constitutional right, and you should exercise it, but to encourage other people to break the law and expect that no consequences will follow is not just being naïve — it is wrong. What will you tell all the other fellow citizens who are behind bars because they felt that some law was unfair and went ahead and broke it? They were not given a pass; otherwise, these fellow Americans would not be behind bars. Do not buy into the narrative that the Europeans just showed up in America and seized Indian lands, therefore, America is a lawless country, and each person can show up and do as they please. It seems you have forgotten that the lands were not handed on a silver platter. Thousands lost their lives in the battles that were fought. Throughout human history, people have moved and occupied lands that others occupied, but it is always a result of conflict, and those that emerge victorious occupy the land. This is not an endorsement of this practice, but I am stating things as they are. How far back do we want to go to redress the history of people occupying the lands of others? You are going to be surprised by how guilty most of the world population is going to be.

If the current wave of immigrants is out to conquer and occupy the lands that they move into by force, they should be ready to fight and not expect the land to be handed to them on a silver platter. If people want peace and prosperity, they MUST be law-abiding first and then look for ways to change or improve the laws. To break laws with impunity and not expect any consequences is a recipe for disaster.

Let us, the people of God, love enough to speak the truth boldly without fear or compromise. The truth and the truth alone will set people free. Why will people run away from countries that have failed them because of lawlessness and move to another country and insist on practicing the same lawlessness that forced them to flee in the first place? When we talk about love, justice, and fairness, it should only be driven by our emotions and how we feel because feelings come and go.

Good laws make the playing field even for all, and if we truly want to be fair and just, everybody must be held to the same standard and to the same set of laws. Encouraging people to break laws because it is the loving and caring thing to do is bizarre, to say the least. We cannot capitulate before those who have perfected the art of name-calling because we dare to call others to obey immigration laws. At the heart of this issue is character — the willingness to die, to live, to surrender, to keep.

These are the core Biblical principles that Jesus taught us, and we should not be afraid to challenge others to embrace and live by these principles because we know that the present suffering is nothing compared to the glory to come. When somebody trains themselves to break the law because things are difficult, they are reinforcing the ability to break the law and, at the same time, weakening the resolve to stand up, take the heat, and develop tenacity and grit. What other laws are these individuals willing to break in the future if the laws get in the way of what they badly need?

We should never forget those who obey the immigration laws paid the price and did it the right way. Let us not call good evil and evil good. It is foolish to look down on those who obeyed the law while exhorting and fighting for those that willfully broke the law. Those that chose to break the laws give many excuses, but none is good enough. They should come clean and accept that they have broken the law, then ask for forgiveness and restoration. Is this not at the heart of the Gospel message?

It is only after somebody has acknowledged, confessed, and forsaken their sin that they will truly be forgiven and restored by God. Therefore, there is no forgiveness without confession, repentance, and forsaking of sin. A Blanket amnesty is not good idea because 1) those who plan to break the law will feel that it is okay to break the law, and 2) those who are law-abiding will feel that obeying the law is not worth it.

What society will survive if laws are not obeyed? If people are rewarded for breaking laws they felt were preventing them from meeting what they considered a legitimate need, what will prevent them from breaking further laws in the future in similar circumstances? There is a process in place to change laws, and everybody must adhere to that, including those who are in need. There is no excuse for not doing what is right, no matter how much we think we can justify it. The fact is that the more you train yourself to do anything, the greater the likelihood that you will repeat it in the future because humans are creatures of habit. Forming the wrong habits and reinforcing them will do you a disservice in the future. Therefore, if we love somebody, we should encourage them to train themselves to develop character and to walk in integrity no matter what. These are qualities that transcend all cultures and have eternal ramifications.

I hope you are getting the point I am trying to make here. Now is the time to act because a lack of engagement will lead to the breakdown of society as we know it. We need to preserve it for our children and the future generation. There is no room for error because the consequences are undesirable. Even if you do not have children or grandchildren, you have to care about the eternal fate of the souls of those that land on our shores, for it is your responsibility, not that of any church or government.

By the way, the government is not an individual – it is a collection of people driven by an agenda. At times, this agenda is diametrically opposed to the direction you, as a child of God, are supposed to be going. You MUST choose to follow the direction toward the kingdom of heaven, of which you are a citizen. You know where the instructions on what you are supposed to be doing are found. If you make it a point of duty to consult the Manual as often as possible, you will do fine.

I am going to get a little more practical on what you can and should be doing to be the salt and light. When it comes to loving God and loving your neighbor as yourself, we must think out of the box because most of what we have done and are still doing is not delivering the desired results. There is no need for any apprehension about what you are going to do. The good news is that we have a role model that we can learn from and move ahead with confidence. Jesus Christ did "ministry" differently from what we are doing today and have been taught to do.

Part of the reason we remain segregated and have a hard time interacting with others is that we have set up our own system to do our own thing in the name of God. Our own preferences are blocking our light and keeping our salt in the salt shaker. Now is the time to get out of the shaker and let your salt come in touch with those that need the salt the most. Remove the traditions of men and cultural preferences and sensitivities so that your light can shine in the darkness. You can do this by doing the following:

Talk to strangers

Most of us were raised and instructed to beware of strangers. This makes a lot of sense for safety reasons, but if we only interact with those that look like us, speak like us and believe like us, we are going to end up with only people that look like us, speak like us and believe like us. Jesus Christ, our role model, understood the importance of talking to strangers and interacting with them even though it was some sort of a taboo. Do you remember the encounter between Jesus Christ and the woman at the well? It is an excellent example of how good things happen when we engage other people genuinely with the desire to make a difference in their lives. As the story goes, Jesus had sent His disciples to a Samaritan village to get some food for them. While the disciples were gone and Jesus was sitting by the well alone, a woman shows up to fetch water. He decided to engage this stranger in the following conversation:

> *A woman of Samaria came to draw water. Jesus said to her, "Give Me a drink." His disciples had gone away into the city to buy food.*
>
> *Then the woman of Samaria said to Him, "How is it that You, being a Jew, ask a drink from me, a Samaritan woman?" For Jews have no dealings with Samaritans.*
>
> *Jesus answered and said to her, "If you knew the gift of God, and who it is who says to you, 'Give Me a drink,' you would have asked Him, and He would have given you living water."* (John 4:7-10 NKJV)

The woman did not expect Jesus to ask her to give Him water. Jews and Samaritans did not mix, but Jesus did not allow this to come between Him and the woman. You see, Jesus cared and loved enough to disregard the social norms to meet the need of this stranger. For you to talk to strangers, you must get out of your comfort zone and talk to people that you meet. Yes, it will be awkward initially, but it will become less uncomfortable as you get used to it. There are many places you meet new people, and you should be open to talking to them. You should use both verbal and non-verbal communication.

Many say people will automatically know that they are followers of Jesus Christ by seeing the way they live. This makes a lot of sense and appeals to sensibilities, but it is not how Jesus Christ conducted Himself. We should follow His lead if we want to get the same results that He got.

When you're on a plane, find common ground to talk to that person sitting next to you. This may be the only time you will ever meet them. Can you tell them what an opportunity it is for the two of you to be sitting together? The reason we do not "disturb" people is because we are not excited enough about the message that we are carrying. Anybody with a cure for cancer will let other people know. We have the cure for sin and should excitedly share it with all who care to listen.

You are going to be surprised by how willing strangers will talk with you if you engage them. Break the ice. Look for something interesting: it can be as simple as the color of their hair or the shoes they are wearing. In the case of the woman at the well, Jesus asked for a drink, and it got her talking and eventually revealed the issues that were in her heart. Like this woman, many will try to cover up the pain, disappointments, and other issues in their lives by trying to argue and be defensive. You can avoid falling into this trap by asking questions and showing genuine interest in people. Your intention is never to win an argument or score any points. All you are trying to do is for an opportunity to point the person to the blessed hope that you have in Christ Jesus. The objective is not to convert them. It is not your responsibility to convict, change, or make anybody to repent — that is the work of the Holy Spirit, not yours.

Many people say they are not outgoing and do not like to talk. I say it depends on the topic. People will get excited about a subject that is dear to them. Your task is to try and figure out what is of interest to the stranger, and the way you do it is by asking questions. You will eventually hit the right nerve, and the person will start talking to you. If you meet the people who will not talk at all no matter how hard you try, you should leave them alone and try again when the right moment presents itself.

One way to break the ice is by offering to give information. Jesus asked for water from the woman, indicating that He was in need. Do not come across as somebody who knows it all and has everything in order. Never forget that you were once a beginner that has found bread and is pointing the road to others so they, too, can find bread. You are not better than anybody else; your righteousness is the righteousness of Christ; and you are saved by grace, not by your works. Therefore, there is no boasting, but giving glory to what Jesus Christ has done for you.

Invite people over for a meal

There is nothing as powerful as having a meal with somebody and having their undivided attention. If the person that you have invited is open enough to accept your invitation, then you are going to have the wonderful privilege of engaging them and getting to know each other better. A lot transpires when people sit together at the table and share a meal. Unfortunately, many consider their houses to be their "private space" and do not want strangers invading it. After all, the church building is the house of God, and all Godly activities must take place in the house of God.

Some wonder, "Why bring people to my house when I can take them to the house of God and let the experts minister to them?" This model has yielded limited results, and we need to change it if we want different results. Right now, most people do not consider their home to be the house of God, too. This has to change because God owns everything that we "have"; we are stewards and have to let God use everything for His glory.

You must have been taught that the "church" is the house of God, and you probably tithed a lot to build the actual church building that you are now fellowshipping in. You give yourself a pat on the back for helping to build the house of God, and now, you can keep your own house to yourself. Why are we equating the modern-day houses of worship to the temple in Jerusalem? If you want to talk about the temple of God, you should not look further than your body because your body has become the temple of God.

Let us take a look at how Jesus used people's houses to reach out to those in need. There was no special lighting, music, or program, but sins were forgiven, and people were healed, delivered, and restored. All these were possible because Jesus had compassion and a genuine interest in helping people. That is how we should be! When you begin to care enough to sit down and listen to other people's stories and interact with them closely, you will see God move in your life in unimaginable ways.

There are many different instances in the Bible, where Jesus was sharing a meal with others but still went ahead to heal and forgive people's sins. It should be noted that the first miracle He performed was at a wedding, not on a crusade. One of the most important activities that the churches do today to remember the death, resurrection, and return of Jesus Christ was instituted during a meal:

And as they were eating, Jesus took bread, blessed and broke it, and gave it to the disciples and said, "Take, eat; this is My body."

Then He took the cup, and gave thanks, and gave it to them, saying, "Drink from it, all of you. For this is My blood of the new covenant, which is shed for many for the remission of sins. But I say to you, I will not drink of this fruit of the vine from now on until that day when I drink it new with you in My Father's kingdom." (Matt. 26:26-29 NKJV)

Can you imagine how Jesus Christ chose to handle such a solemn occasion? He did not go to some special temple or retreat hall to institute this important practice that will be commemorated for thousands of generations and even throughout eternity because, based on His words, we will drink of the cup and eat the bread with Him in heaven.

Other crucial things transpired during that meal, including the issue of who was going to betray Him. Don't you think it would have been more appropriate if Jesus had preached at a service to deliver that powerful convicting sermon? No. He decided to have a meal with His disciples and shared it there. It was also during this meal that Jesus washed the feet of His disciples to demonstrate to them how a servant leader should relate to those under his leadership.

After the death and resurrection of Jesus, we still see meals playing an important role in His ministry. On the way to Emmaus, He was invited by two disciples to pass the night with them. Jesus had been explaining the scriptures to them while they were walking, but it is when Jesus took bread, gave thanks, and broke it that the eyes of the disciples were opened, and they recognized Him. On another occasion, we find Him by the lake of Galilee roasting fish for the disciples shortly before He ascended to heaven.

Opening your house to immigrants and sharing a meal with them is the most powerful way to share the love of Christ. There is a lot that can be done to make this visit fruitful. Why not display the Ten Commandments in your house? This can initiate a spiritual conversation. The big advantage is that when somebody accepts the invitation to come over for a meal, they will give you their undivided attention. You are not going to use a big bat to beat the Gospel into them. Instead, you will have ample opportunity to share your home and your testimony.

Start by asking them to share their own stories. Many people like to share their stories, especially immigrants who have braved all and abandoned a lot to move to a new country. It is only fair that after allowing them to share, they, too, will be willing to listen to your story. The question for you is, do you know your own story? You have one, and it is powerful. In short, everybody has a powerful story. The efficacy of your story is in the telling, not its substance.

There is nothing more effective than having somebody over and sharing a meal at your dining table. We are living in a time when fewer and fewer people make home meals and eat out more. This is driven by convenience, and the objective for some is to save time and money. While this makes sense to us, it is time to make some drastic changes if it is hampering the very mission that God has for you. You may have to have that meal once a month in your house during which you invite an immigrant or immigrant family to connect with you and share each other's stories. You do not need to prepare a gourmet meal, and your home does not need to be impeccable for somebody to come over and visit. Practicing hospitality should not require a lot of preparation. What really matters and will make a huge difference is the love and warm heart that you have for people. This is the reason why you must pray for a heart of love and compassion for others, especially those who are different from you and have come from different countries.

There are many ample opportunities to have people over. Why not invite them during Thanksgiving and share the Thanksgiving story with them? It will be very appropriate and fitting to present the Christian version of that story. Many newly-arrived immigrants do not have anybody to spend Thanksgiving with because it is an American holiday. Why not make it a tradition to invite a colleague at work or reach out to a university and invite an international student? I was an international student at one point in my life, and those early Thanksgivings that I spent with American families left a mark on my life. We cannot allow the desire for convenience to get in the way of the most important responsibility that God has given us to do. The 4th of July weekend is another great opportunity to engage immigrants because many do not have anybody to celebrate with. It is a great opportunity to reach out and invite them over for a barbecue or to go out and watch the fireworks.

There are going to be some challenges as you invite people, especially immigrants, over to your house for a meal. But don't let this scare you and prevent you from doing so. The risk of not having them over is far greater because the eternal destiny of the souls of these immigrants, if they are not yet followers of Jesus, is at stake.

I am going to share with you three different incidents that occurred in my own house when we had guests over for a meal.

The first case was that of a friend who is a practicing Baha'i. We had invited them to come over for a meal, and while we sat at the table to eat, I asked one of our children to say grace before the meal. Immediately after our child finished praying, our guest interjected a Baha'i prayer. We were completely surprised by this, but we did not say anything. We proceeded to share the meal and had a wonderful time. This particular incident is ingrained in my mind. Our guest was bold and comfortable enough to express his beliefs, even though they were different from ours. How many of us followers of Christ are bold witnesses for Him, especially when the conditions are not conducive? We shy behind all sorts of reasons and excuses because we do not want to be embarrassed. If Jesus Christ is truly who He says He is —God in the flesh, the only way to God, the person through whom everything was made, His name is above all principalities and powers of things in heaven and under the earth— then we must be proud that we know Him and that He calls us by name. Do not allow the devil to use fear and shame to steal your witness.

The second incident was when we invited a Muslim family over for a meal at our house. When they arrived, and the food was served, they asked if we used any pork or pork products. We told them that there was no pork in the food and no pork products in the house. We have been around Muslims enough to know that they do not eat pork, and it would not have made any sense to prepare pork that day. If you are a pork lover, surely you can sacrifice one meal. Their soul is more important than a juicy tenderloin, so give up that tenderloin for that day and be a good host. The sacrifice is worth it. Do all you can to make your guest comfortable. You may be asking: what about me? Nothing about you! Let the example of Jesus Christ, who left heaven, came down on earth and suffered on your behalf, be enough motivation for you to sacrifice some of your comforts and delights to do His work.

Back to our guests, Muslim family. When we finished eating and sat down to catch up and get to know each other better, the husband said it was time for them to pray and asked if it was okay to pray in our living room. I proposed that the husband use one of our bedrooms, and he complied. By the time we were figuring out where his wife could pray, she had taken matters in her own hands and went down on her knees on one section of our living room and started praying. We did not interfere with her prayer, and when she and her husband were done praying, we continued our visit. We explained to our children later on what transpired and taught them a little about the Muslim faith. We were not mad at what happened. Instead, we were challenged by the boldness and courage of this couple. They did not care where they were and what we would think of them because their devotion to Allah is more important. It was not something that they only spoke about — they lived it. How many of us followers of Jesus Christ are ashamed to pray in restaurants because we do not want to look odd? Isn't it sad that we talk more about movie stars and sports stars than our Lord Jesus Christ? May God help us to wake up and stand with Him. We serve a mighty God who is mightier than any other god. He will protect us, so do not be afraid to bring people over to your house just because they might pray to a different god.

We invited another couple to have dinner with us, and after we had finished eating, we started talking. Our guest asked if, in Cameroon, wild animals like monkeys, chickens, gorillas roam the city streets. The question jolted me a bit. I decided that this was an educational moment, so I asked one of my children to get my iPad. I Googled Yaounde, the capital of Cameroon, and showed our guest how the city looks, pointing to the fact that there was no wildlife on the streets, but cars and people like any other modern city. Our guest was surprised that Yaounde has tarred roads, congested traffic, street lights, and high-rise buildings. The pictures and my explanation illuminated their minds and helped to correct the distortion our guest had about Cameroon and Africa, in general. We did not argue. There was no need for me to be upset and offended because what my guest needed was unbiased information about my country and continent of birth. Google helped to provide that, and in the end, their stereotypes about Africa were corrected.

When you invite immigrants over for a meal and engage them in conversation, you will be surprised by the biases, misinformation, and stereotypes that you personally hold about other countries. You can hear information directly from primary sources, which may be different from some of the distorted and agenda-driven programming you have been accustomed to watching on television and reading in the newspapers.

The immigrants themselves have their own biases, stereotypes, and misinformation that must be corrected as well. And the best place to do this is by sitting down and connecting with immigrants over a meal and having two-way conversations.

Most of the information that people from other parts of the world know about the United States of America is controlled and heavily influenced by Hollywood. It is portrayed as a land of plenty; everybody is rich and well-off. Therefore, there is no poverty in America, and everybody has money to spare. People are not told about credit card debt, student loans, mortgages, and the high cost of living, plus all the state and federal taxes that must be paid. No wonder when I first got here, I could not understand why most of those I was interacting with were complaining about not having money, but were living in big houses and driving fancy cars. As time went on, I got a firsthand education on the role debt plays in the American way of life. This was a rude awakening and fundamentally changed my perspective about the country and her people.

We cannot wait for the government to legislate who comes over for a meal on our dinner table. Inviting people of all ethnicities and backgrounds will deal a fatal blow to segregation. I watched the movie *All Saints*[14] directed by Steve Gomer, and it vividly portrayed some of what we are discussing here. I strongly recommend that you watch it if you have not already done so. The movie is based on a true story about a group of immigrants that fled Myanmar, formerly known as Burma, to resettle in Smyrna, Tennessee. These refugees had little knowledge

---

[14]   *All Saints*, directed by Steve Gomer (Affirm Films, 2017), DVD (DVD, 2017).

of the English language and were struggling to fit into the community. Michael Spurlock, an Episcopalian priest, is sent to Smyrna to sell the All Saints Church because it only had twenty-five members and was struggling to pay its mortgage. What ensues is a drama of epic proportions because the church opened its doors to about seventy of the Burmese refugees, which led to many different cultural clashes. How they resolved them is something that you need to watch the movie to understand.

I want to note one particular incident that is directly related to the subject of inviting people over for a meal. One of the members of All Saints was a Vietnam war veteran. He went to visit one of the refugees but did not enter their house even though they invited him to come in. The family was having a meal, and the church member preferred to go sit in his truck and wait for them to finish eating. The refugee family put aside his own share of the food and took it to the car, and gave it to him. Thank God that he did not refuse the food.

As you invite people over to eat, they may bring food with them or invite you to come and eat with them as well. If you do not have any food allergies, you are going to learn how to eat some of the same things that you have been used to eating but prepared differently. Learning how to be polite, not make faces, and accepting will help to break down barriers and bridge differences.

Take, for example, corn, rice, and potatoes are eaten all over the world but prepared differently by different ethnicities. Some make corn powder, add sugar, milk, and eggs and bake it. Others mix the cornflour with pepper, onions, and other vegetables, wrap it and boil instead of baking. These two corn-based dishes will look different and taste different, but one is not superior to the other. The bottom line is that you are taking in carbohydrates that will provide energy to your body. The same goes for how beef, pork, fish, vegetables are prepared differently by different ethnicities. Only the uninformed will surmise that their own method of preparing vegetables, beef, pork, etc. is superior. The question is, how one method is superior? It is sad that ethnocentrism is extended to food, drink, and other aspects of our lives that are supposed to unite and bring us together. I think Paul the apostle understood this when he gave the following instructions:

Eat whatever is sold in the meat market, asking no questions for conscience' sake; for the earth is the Lord's, and all its fullness.

If any of those who do not believe invites you to dinner, and you desire to go, eat whatever is set before you, asking no question for conscience' sake. But if anyone says to you, "This was offered to idols," do not eat it for the sake of the one who told you, and for conscience' sake; for "the earth is the Lord's, and all its fullness." "Conscience" I say, not your own, but that of the other. For why is my liberty judged by another man's conscience? But if I partake with thanks, why am I evil spoken of for the food over which I give thanks?

Therefore, whether you eat or drink, or whatever you do, do all to the glory of God. Give no offense, either to the Jews or to the Greeks or to the church of God, just as I also please all men in all things, not seeking my own profit, but the profit of many, that they may be saved. (1 Cor. 10:25-33 NKJV)

The long and short of it is that when invited to eat somewhere, eat and do not make a big deal about the food unless you have health-related restrictions. Never allow your personal preferences to hamper the Gospel because the eternal destiny of somebody's soul is more important than trying to satisfy your taste buds or quench your thirst. As simple as this may sound, a lot of people struggle with eating in other people's houses, especially those that are culturally different from them, because they are not sure of what they are being served, and they fear being harmed by the food. At times, these fears are driven by deep-rooted prejudices based on distorted information about other cultures. We have to educate ourselves enough to know that food is for the stomach and the stomach is for food,. To be able to interact at this level, it is going to take trust and acceptance that they, too, are made in the image and likeness of God.

In the fifteen years I have lived in the United States of America, I can testify that I have seen this at work firsthand because two people have embraced us. Each time they come over for a meal, they eat and have never complained about the food that we serve them. Some of the food items are tropical. They had never seen or eaten the items before, but they embraced it and liked it as well. The level of interaction we are advocating here is going beyond just inviting somebody over and treating it as some sort of project. You have to genuinely love them and allow the Holy Spirit to do the work of conviction and transformation. All you are required to do is to share the Gospel when appropriate.

This subject of having meals at home is not complete without mentioning the good work of Truett Austin and his wife Karen, who made it a point of duty to come and pick us up and another couple when we were newly-arrived international students at the University of Texas at Dallas. He would show up during the weekend on Saturday evening and take us to his house for us to have a meal, talk and swim. This was so refreshing, relaxing, and took our minds off our books and helped us to cope with homesickness. We had the opportunity to enjoy homemade American cuisine and delicacies. After dinner, we played board games and had a lot of meaningful conversations centered around our countries, the United States of America, the state of the church, and world politics. These exchanges were informative, enriching, and educational. We got to know each other better, and the openness and acceptance from this couple made a lot of difference in our lives. The bonding and the friendship were deepened enough to the point that after more than fifteen years, we are still friends, we check on each other often, and we still get together to share meals and talk.

This is just one example of many stories that I can share of people who reached out to us when we first arrived in the United States and invited us over for Thanksgiving to have lunch together. There is no space here to name all the people that participated in transitioning us into our new life in the US. The point I am trying to make here is that the opportunity to engage others is there, and many more people should get involved. When people arrive in any country, the first couple of months are crucial because they have many needs. Most of them are clueless about many things and have many misconceptions that need to be corrected. This is the perfect time to reach out to them and make a positive impression that will go a long way in shaping and influencing the rest of their stay in the country. The most common complaint is lack of time, but the truth is that this is not a priority to us. We have created time for all the other "important" things in our lives. Unfortunately, the eternal destinies of many people are at the bottom of our to-do list. I hope that you will reevaluate your agendas and change it for the better.

Engage in outdoor activities

Many immigrants desire to know how to live in the United States of America and fit into society. For this to happen, somebody that was either born here or has lived here long enough and knows what to do should engage them. There are many outdoor activities like hiking, camping, hunting, fishing, kayaking, etc. that many immigrants would like to do but are clueless on how to go about it. Do not forget that most of these immigrants feel like a "tree" that has been uprooted and replanted and is trying to reestablish its roots. This is a difficult process, and any help that can be given to them is welcomed.

Many of these things may be taken for granted by you because you were born in this country and often assume that everybody else knows them. This is an assumption that has to change. Most immigrants move to big cities, and the demands of living in such cities make it difficult for them to disengage and get involved in some of these outdoor activities. The few that desire to are clueless about where to start. Please do not tell me that they should just Google it and figure out what to do. It is not that simple. Did you Google about your first camping trip and just got up and did it? Even if you did, do not forget that when people move from one country to another, there are so many new things for them to learn that it gets overwhelming. Therefore, any help that can be given to them will be gladly received. You can be part of the solution.

For many years, my family desired to go camping, and we reached out to a few people and requested that they take us out and show us the ropes, but it did not work out. People are busy and afraid that it may be a liability to take others out to go camping. As good as this sounds, with proper preparation and the right education, it can be done. If you camp regularly, you should reach out to some immigrants who are interested and get them involved. Can you imagine how much information you will share sitting around a campfire and the ample opportunities to share the Gospel that may come up?

We have been told that the church is a building, and we must meet there every Sunday for service, and this will please God. Many of us have bought into this narrative, and our lives revolve around the building and all the activities that take place there. According to this setup, you have to show up as often as possible to be "spiritual." Perfect attendance is a measure of the degree of your seriousness and commitment. What are you committed to? How does attending church service help the cause of the Gospel if all it does is for you to get more head knowledge and have a good time? Have you thought about what you have done with all the sermons, Bible studies, and Sunday School lessons you have attended year in and year out? Eating is just part of the equation; exercising is the other crucial part of growth. How can we measure our spiritual growth by the amount of spiritual food that we are eating? Have you heard that faith without works is dead?

This message is for you as an individual, and it is not a call for another church program or function. There is nothing wrong with church programs and functions, they have their place, but for us to make disciples of all the nations, ALL of us must roll up our sleeves and get involved in building personal relationships with people and sharing the Gospel at the individual level. One of the ways is going out camping, fishing, or any other outdoor activities with people who desperately need the Gospel. Do not forget that God allowed you to be here on earth not only for you to have fun but to be used by Him to establish His kingdom through your witness and making disciples of all nations.

Be a mentor

It is staggering how many immigrants need mentors to help them navigate the complexities of life in a foreign country. These immigrants have too many questions that need answers, and anybody who steps up to the plate to offer some of these answers will be fostering the growth of trust. Over the years, I have reached out to a couple of people and asked to be mentored, but it has not been possible because people were either busy or they did not know what to do. All I needed was to meet once in a while, ask some questions and learn the ropes about living and succeeding in the United States of America. Nobody is superhuman, and when you move into a different country, there is a lot that you do not know and need to know; you may not even know you need to know about them.

I will never forget Mr. Patrick Lowry, who passed suddenly in February 2016. He was instrumental in my professional career as a geologist because he took an interest in me and gave me the necessary feedback and advice that I needed. While I was a student, I attended the Dallas Geological Society meetings regularly. One day, he invited me to his office and suggested a couple of books and resources that I should be reading if I was interested in joining the oil and gas industry after graduation. When I graduated, I got my first job in the oil and gas industry. After one year, the economic downturn of 2008 negatively impacted the oil and gas industry to the point where thousands of workers, including myself, were laid off by the company. Back then, I was an international with an H1-B visa. This meant that to remain legal in the United States of America, I needed somebody to give me a job, or I go back to school and become a student. Since the economy was bad and there were few jobs in the oil and gas industry, companies preferred hiring American workers to people on H1-B visas like myself because they were required by law to justify why the job was not offered to an American worker. This meant that my chances of getting a job were nil.

While in school and at the same time praying on what to do, I paid to learn how to use one of the crucial software that geologists used on a daily basis to do their work. Right up to this point, I had worked in the oil and gas industry in the service sector as a field engineer, not as a geologist. This meant that I had to retool myself to be employed as a geologist. Attending the course to learn how to use this software for two days was not enough for me to become proficient enough to use the software. This is when my mentor stepped in and helped me out.

At that time, he was the head of a consulting firm and invited me to come and practice using the software in his office so that I could gain some experience. He could not legally pay me, and the company was not in a position to employ me because I did not have the experience necessary to do that level of technical consulting. Therefore, I was given an office, real data, and resources to hone my skills in using the software. We would go out for lunch, and he would coach me on what to expect in corporate America and how to be a successful geologist. He was blunt, straightforward, and did not cut any corners when he engaged me in any conversation. In the beginning, it was uncomfortable, but I knew he had my best interest at heart. As time went on, we truly got to know each other better, and I appreciated every moment we spent together.

I remember one particular day when I just started working there, he walked in and I was sitting at my desk and trying to appear busy because I thought that was the appropriate thing to do. He schooled me on what I should do and how I should conduct myself in the future when my boss walks into my office. I had many deficiencies, and he helped me to overcome them. Some of these were technical; some were social. You may be wondering why I was struggling in some of these areas. Do not be surprised: I was not born and raised in the United States of America, and I had a lot to learn. Some of the things that are culturally appropriate in the culture that I was raised in are a liability in the American culture, and I needed somebody to help me adjust to my new reality. For example, in Cameroon, you are not expected to look into the eyes of your elders when you talk to them. This is considered rude and disrespectful. But in this country, if you are talking with somebody and avoiding eye contact, it is considered to be a sign of lack of confidence on your part or that you may be hiding something.

It is important to understand all these challenges so that the immigrants who have moved into the country from other parts of the world can be helped to grow and fit in. Somebody has to reach out to them and teach them what to do. Otherwise, they will make mistakes not because they want to, but because they do not know any better. These immigrants are here to stay, and the future of the country depends on them as well. Therefore, the prudent thing to do is to equip them to do well. Mentorship is one of the ways this can be done. Again, I am not referring to some organized and formal mentorship programs. Rather, it is a call to individuals to take it upon themselves to seek opportunities to connect with others and mentor them. Mr. Patrick Lowry is an excellent example of what I am talking about. Nobody asked him to mentor me, and he was not doing it under the auspices of any organization. Everything that he did for me came from the heart. It was beautiful and meaningful.

Another great mentor is Dr. James Carter. I met him at the University of Texas at Dallas when I first arrived as an international student without any money or scholarships and was still trying to figure out what to do. I had too many questions and very few answers. He was always willing to listen and give much-needed advice, and his wisdom flowed to me. He went above and beyond what was expected to smooth out the rough patches that I encountered here. He has become a part of our family, and the relationship has grown stronger over the years. We have shared so many wonderful moments in and out of the house.

Another mentor of mine is Earl Little. I met him in church during my second year in the United States of America. He, too, took an interest in me and has been very instrumental in my spiritual life. Through him, I met Dave Dawson, director and founder of Equipping the Saints, an organization that helps to connect the dots on the fulfillment of the Great Commission, obeying the great commandment and living a life of obedience. Meeting Dave is one of the greatest things that has happened in my life since I moved to the United States of America. In fact, this book is a result of that. He ignited in me the passion for calling every saint to join in Mission Dei, and he handed me the tools needed to do that. Uncle Earl, as we fondly call him, is still a big part of our lives. We have shared so many memories and have done a lot of ministry-related activities and will continue doing them as long as the Lord keeps us alive. He currently serves on the board of Equipping the Saints International Ministries.

As you can see, I am not a self-made individual. Many other people have poured their lives into mine and continue to do so. It is a fact that my life would not have been what it is if these men I mentioned did not do what they did and continue to do what they are doing. When I need help, advice, or counsel, I call them, and they let me talk and bounce my ideas off them. I thank God for bringing these men into my life and for using them to sharpen me.

If you are reading this book and currently not mentoring anybody, please pray and do something about it. There are thousands of immigrants in this country that need a lot of help, and you can make a difference. If you are already mentoring somebody, God bless you. Let this be an encouragement for you to continue with the good work. You may not see your results right now, but in due season, you will be amazed by what God will do through the seeds that you are sowing. I was thanking my mentors for all the time and resources that they have invested in my life over the years, and I like to point out to them that their investment did not fail; it has yielded some fruit and will continue to do so in the foreseeable future.

Host an international student

This is an excellent opportunity that has been utilized over the years by many Christians in the United States of America to help international students transition into their new lives in America. An organization that comes to mind is the International Students, Inc. (ISI). They believe in "making a difference a student at a time."[15] They have numerous resources on their website, and in many different ways, you can get involved. Here are some sobering statistics from their website that should make any mission-minded individual think twice. It is estimated that 75% of all international students that come to the United States of America to attend school will never enter an American home while in the US. An even higher number of 80% of the international students will never enter a church building while in the United States of America. In 2017, about 1.18 million international students came to the United States of America to study.[16]

Many of these students are from China, Saudi Arabia, and many other countries that are not open to the Gospel. To the United States of America and other western countries, sending these students for

---

[15] "Get Involved," International Students, Inc., http://www.isionline.org/Home.aspx (accessed April 1, 2018).

[16] Beckie Smith, "US: international students top 1.18 million," The Pie News: News and Business Analysis for Preofessionals in International Education, July 7, 2017, https://thepienews.com/news/usa-international-students-1-18-million-sevis-by-the-numbers-2017/ (accessed April 1, 2018).

further education is an indication that they want the good things that the West has to offer. The foundation of western civilization is their Judeo-Christian heritage, and we should not be ashamed to share that with these students. These so-called closed societies can be penetrated when we reach these students with the Gospel and disciple them enough for them to become ambassadors of Christ when they go back home. Anybody who has encountered the saving power of our Lord Jesus Christ is changed forever. These students who are going to be potential leaders in their respective countries because of the doors an American degree opens will also become ambassadors of Jesus Christ and will take the Gospel into their closed countries. We have to stop trying to be the only ones who have to go and start entrusting the Gospel into the hands of others, believing that the same God who is at work in us will work in them and accomplish His mission of reconciling the world to Himself. The West has been at the forefront of evangelizing the world for many years, but God is doing a new thing by bringing the "mission field" to us. We cannot turn a blind eye to the more than one million international students that come to the United States of America each year. Now is the time to open your home and your life for God to bring in some of these international students so you can share His love with them.

Some people allow these students to live in their houses for a few months before moving into their own apartments. Do you have an empty room in your house? Why are you wasting space? There is a student out there who will be more than happy to spend a week or two in your home. During that time, you can sow some seeds that will go a long way. When students come here initially, they have many questions and needs, and those that reach out to them have a great opportunity to make a lifelong impact. If you do not want the students to live in your house, it is okay to invite them over for a meal, Thanksgiving, Christmas, or any other holiday. Many students want to learn about the United States and the American way of life, and the people of God should be at the forefront of making this happen. We, as a country, must be interested in international students because not all of them go back when they graduate. Some end up like me: getting jobs here and becoming citizens.

The emphasis in this chapter has been on the need to act now, and I presented various ways through which you can act now. I focused solely on immigrants that are not yet believers in the Lord Jesus Christ, but this does not mean that all immigrants who come into the country do not have a personal relationship with Christ. Some of the immigrants are already believers, and God has called some of them to this country to participate in God's mission of sharing the Gospel and making disciples of those in the West. We need to reach out to them and help them accomplish this important mission. They need resources, encouragement, and partnerships that will complement some of the lapses that they may be having.

Most missionary organizations prepare their people before sending them out, and while they are on the mission field, the home base sends supplies and resources. This is not the case with most of the immigrants from developing countries who are involved in making disciples of all the nations. Most of the developing countries have this distorted belief that there is a lot of money in the West, and money can only flow from the West to the developing countries. Because of this, those who are here receive little or no support from their countries of origin. It is important to understand this and factor it in as you interact with our brethren from other parts of the world who are involved in the Mission Dei in our midst.

Now is the time for you to get involved. You do not need some special government or church programs to reach out to other immigrants and make a difference in their lives. As Max Lucado said, "If you have a sandwich, you can practice hospitality." You already know that we are called to live by faith, and it is going to take faith for you to do any of the things that have been suggested here. The next chapter is going to be a call for us to walk by faith and not by sight.

Conclusion:
Now Is the Time

You are probably wondering how on earth you are going to respond to the challenge that has been presented to you concerning Mission Dei about the immigrants in our midst. I commend you for reading this far — it is a sure indication that you have taken this subject seriously enough and have invested the time necessary to learn about it. You may be worried about the risk involved in talking to strangers and inviting people you do not know into your home, even going on camping or hunting trips with them. What if you go out and something bad happened? What about issues of liability if people come over for a meal and somebody gets sick from the food you served? Some of the horror stories you have heard maybe screaming at you right now. All you hear is, "NO! NO! NO! Don't do it! Why do you want to jeopardize your current lifestyle? By the way, you already do a lot at church, and your plate is too full to add one more thing." You may still be telling yourself that the professional clergy is there to take care of all this ministry stuff and that you do not have what it takes to share the Gospel and disciple the nations. Besides, God is already using other people to do it, and if God wanted you to be involved, He would tell you.

First of all, God does not call the qualified. He calls people and then qualifies them, empowers them, and does His work through them. Therefore, the excuse of not being qualified does not hold. You are more than qualified because you are a priest of God. This also addresses the belief that the "professional clergy" is charged with the responsibility of taking care of the spiritual things, while you go and do your own thing and pay your tithes and offerings. This is not what the new covenant teaches. It is a new day, there is a new High Priest in town, and the orders have changed drastically. Jesus Christ is our new High Priest, and you are His priest. He expects you to carry out your priestly duties wherever you are. In addition to being a priest, your body has become the temple of the Holy Spirit. The implication of this is that God no longer dwells in buildings but is with you everywhere and always. Let the presence of God in you bring light into the darkness that is surrounding you.

Secondly, waiting for God to speak again when He has already spoken is putting the Lord to the test because you have not obeyed the first instructions, and yet, you need more. What about "Love God with all your heart and love your neighbor as yourself" do you not understand? Do you need the instruction about going into all the world and making disciples of all the nations to be given again? The great commandment has already been passed, and the great commission issued. All of us, including you, must step out in faith and start obeying these instructions if we want to live a life of obedience. There is no neutral ground: we are either living in obedience or disobedience. It is not left to us to pick and choose which commandment to obey. By the way, the Bible is summed up in these two commandments. The way we show that we are living a life of obedience is by participating in the great commission.

Do not freak out because you are being called to participate in God's mission of reconciling the world through Jesus Christ. It is not you who is going to do the work; Christ, working through you by the power of the Holy Spirit, will draw people unto Himself when you lift Him up. You are called upon to walk by faith and not by sight, and it is going to require you to trust God and obey. Your feelings will not take you far. What you have to do is to put your trust in the Lord and His word, and you will be able to do what He has already called you to do, and He has all the resources that you need for this crucial assignment.

God is not the author of confusion and does not place us in situations He knows we cannot handle. You are in the right place at the right time, and God is not surprised by world events or political upheavals and the massive displacement and movements of people. It may appear that the devil is winning, but we know that God always has the last laugh, and He is going to. Let us have faith enough to believe in the sovereignty of God and trust Him to make use of the good, the bad, and the ugly that may be associated with all the changes that are associated with the influx of immigrants.

You know why you are the right person for the job and why now is the right time to get involved because if you do not, who else will? The need is great, and we cannot afford not to do something about it because the future of our country depends on how well the immigrants get assimilated and equipped to become productive members of society. In addition to the peace and prosperity of the country, the most important factor that should drive you to engage the immigrant population is the eternal destiny of their souls. This is something that is of top priority in the heart of your heavenly Father because He sent His only-begotten Son, our Lord Jesus Christ, to come and die on the cross to save all who call out to Him. Now is the time for you to take this wonderful news to those who are in need. Let the love that you have for God motivate you to do that, not grudgingly but joyfully and without complaint. You will gain an eternal reward.

Thank you for sticking to the end. We have an entire country and people's souls to save, so let's get to work.

Acknowledgments

Iwill start by thanking my heavenly Father for taking the first step towards me when I was lost in my transgression. He continues to reveal His wonderful plans for me. Lately, He has impressed in my heart very strongly the need to share this good news of the kingdom with other people and equip them to do the same.

Without the Godly example of my parents, I would not have this burning passion for the kingdom of God. My parents did not only talk about the need for me and my siblings to have faith in God, but they also demonstrated to us what it means to love God. They were able to open a couple of churches while doing their regular professions. Now, I understand that to participate in God's mission, you do not need to quit your job. God placed you in that job because He wants you to be light and salt there.

There have been numerous spiritual mentors in my life, and there isn't enough room here to name them, but Dr. Bisong David was the first person who took the ministry of equipping the saints seriously enough to pour his life into mine and other leaders while I was an undergraduate student.

A special thank you to Dave Dawson, who helped me connect the dots by disciplining me and equipping me to disciple others. He is a man who went all out for Mission Dei and has left an eternal impact upon my life.

I also want to thank Earl Little for living the message in this book. When I arrived in the United States of America almost two decades ago, we met at Hillcrest Church, and he took a genuine interest in me. He has been a source of great inspiration, encouragement, and help. He currently serves on the Board of our Equipping of the Saints International Ministry.

A special thank you to Dr. Collins and Ruth Collins, former missionaries to Cameroon, who not only picked me up at the airport but gave me accommodation for my first two nights in the US.

Ray Cotton and all the International Christian Fellowship (ICF) staff and volunteers that serve students of the University of Texas at Dallas must be commended for all they did for me and continue to do for other international students. I had been sleeping on the floor of my student room for a few days when he showed up with a bed just for me. I will never forget that act of kindness.

Truett Austin and his wife opened not only their lives, but their home became my home away from home.

Thank you to Dr. Samuel Ekuwe, originally from Nigeria, but now a US citizen, who understands the need to be part of the Mission Dei and was instrumental in being there for us in our hour of greatest need.

Without the diligence of my editorial team, this work would not have been possible. For that, I am extremely grateful. A big thank you to the design team at IEM Press for a job well done.

To you, my reading audience, you are the reason I keep writing, and I want to thank you for your continuous support and encouragement.

About the Author

Dr. Eric Tangumonkem is a geoscientist, author, speaker, coach, professor, and an entrepreneur. He was born and raised in Cameroon, Africa. As a young adult, he migrated to the United States of America. He has a Doctorate degree in Geosciences from the University of Texas at Dallas and is a professor at Missional University, Embry Riddle, and West Hills College.

As President of IEM Approach, a premier personal growth and leadership development company, Dr. Tangumonkem's mission is to inspire, equip, and motivate people from all walks of life to discover God's-potential in them, live it, and maximize their giftedness. To do this, the growth and development of the body, mind, and spirit MUST be in synergy. He has published several books and resources on personal growth and development and conducts public workshops, coaching, and custom training programs for companies and organizations worldwide.

If you want to invite Dr. Tangumonkem to come and speak at your event, please call 317-975-0806 or email eternalkingdom101@gmail.com.

You can also follow him on social media
Twitter: @DrTangumonkem
Facebook: drtangumonkem
Email: dr.tangumonkem@gmail.com

Available for speaking engagements:

If you want to invite Dr. Tangumonkem to come and speak you can all him using this number 317-975-0806 or email him at eternalkingdom101@gmail.com

Other Resources by the Author

Why I Refused to Become an Illegal Alien: Navigating the Complexities of the American Immigration System

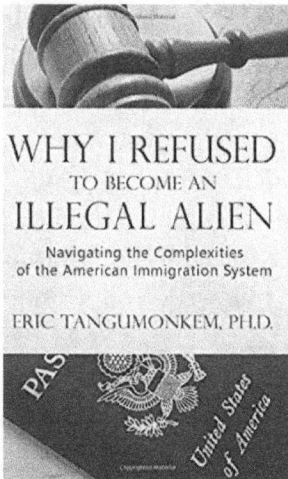

When it comes to the problem of illegal immigration, divisive rhetoric has shut out the voice of reason and common sense. Polarization has resulted in two extreme views--either open the borders wide and allow the free movement of people and goods, or close the borders and prevent people from coming in. The solution is somewhere in the middle . . . if we are willing to listen to one another. Why I Refused to Become an Illegal Alien chronicles the long and arduous journey of one man who immigrated legally and believes that the cost of allowing America's present immigration crisis to remain unresolved is too high. Drawing upon his deep Judeo-Christian roots, this newly-naturalized US citizen sets forth Bible-based solutions that emphasize the need to be our brother's keeper--to show love, mercy, and compassion and at the same time be fair and just.

Make Yourself at Home: An Immigrant's Guide to Settling in America

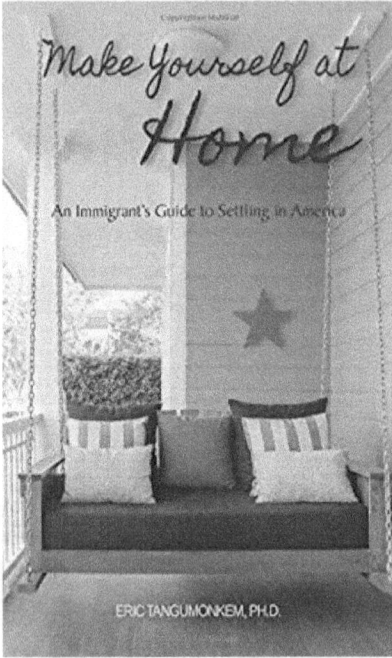

We live in a fallen world plagued by political unrest, conflicts, and wars. These factors, coupled with the desire for a better life, compel people to move to other areas—even across continents and oceans. Immigration brings people face to face with diverse cultures, and wherever diverse cultures meet, either there is immense personal growth, or things can go south quickly. The strategies introduced in this book are for immigrants who are new to the United States of America, but they are applicable to anyone who migrates within or outside of a country. Make Yourself at Home is a valuable resource for helping immigrants avoid the pitfalls experienced by those who have gone before them. Author Eric Tangumonkem, himself an immigrant and naturalized American citizen, presents practical assimilation strategies for education, money, home life, community, and health that, if followed, will position immigrants to excel in their new home.

8

Coming to America: A Journey of Faith

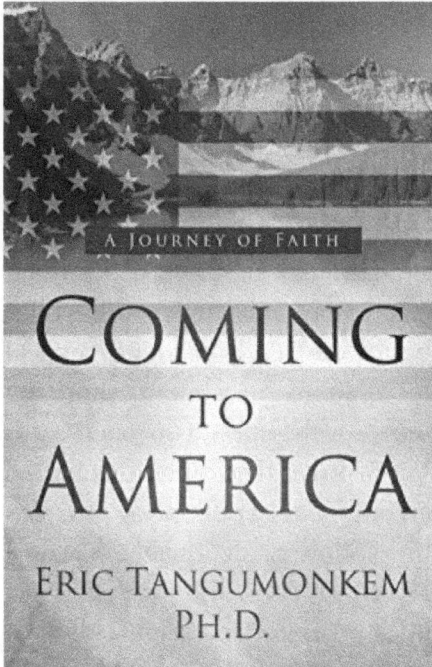

Do you struggle with trusting God with your finances? Feel that God is calling you to do something big but you can't see how it will be accomplished? Fear that He has abandoned you after starting your journey of faith? Coming to America: A Journey of Faith is Eric Tangumonkem's story of wrestling with these thoughts and doubts. God called him to America from Cameroon to pursue graduate studies at the University of Texas at Dallas, but he had no money to put towards this dream. In this book, Tangumonkem shares his journey of learning to trust God as he stepped out in faith and came to America despite a lack of funds. He also shares some of his formative experiences prior to this call-experiences that will encourage readers in their faith. Tangumonkem's life is a testimony to the faithfulness of God, and he is careful to give Him all of the glory.

The Use and Abuse of Titles in The Church

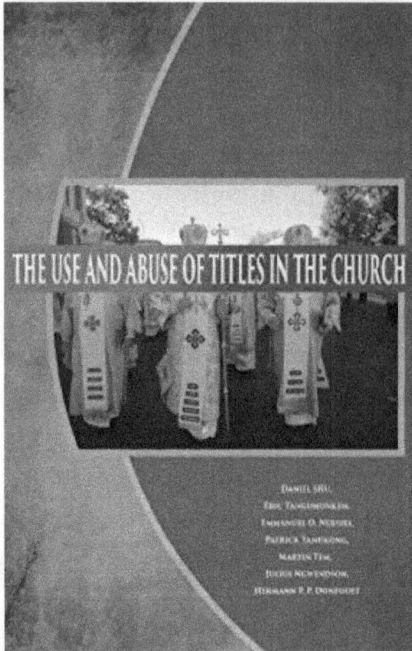

This book examines reasons behind the disturbing proliferation of titles in Christendom in recent times by seven distinguished Christian professionals. The book challenges readers to stay on the straight and narrow road, which celebrates ministers with titles bestowed based on sound Biblical foundations, while shunning those with titles associated with self-promotion and doctrinal errors. The book also provides the following actionable insights: How to identify the proper use of titles A history on the use of titles in Christendom How to avoid the pitfalls of acquiring bogus titles An understanding of the relationship between titles and leadership

Seven Success Keys Learned From My Father

SEVEN SUCCESS KEYS
LEARNED FROM MY FATHER

ERIC TANGUMONKEM., PH.D.

This is a book about my father, my teacher, my role model and hero. A man of passion like any other man, but a man of exceptional qualities and abilities as well. The following are the seven keys to success my father passed to me: Fear of God, Humility, Education, Integrity, Hard work, Prayer and Vision. All these keys have been instrumental in making me who I am today. In addition to these keys, my father was present when we were growing up. He made it a point of duty to talk the talk and walk the walk before us. This book illustrates how these seven keys to success were interwoven in our day-to-day lives and how they have opened unprecedented doors of success to me. My sincere prayer for you as you read this book is that these keys will open all doors for you and bring the success you desire so strongly. Amen!

Viajando a América: Un Camino de Fe (Spanish Edition)

¿Lucha con confiar en Dios con sus finanzas? Siente que Dios le está llamando a hacer algo grande, pero usted no puede ver la forma en que se llevará a cabo? ¿Teme a que Él le ha abandonado después de comenzar su camino de fe?

Viajando a América: Un Camino de Fe es la historia de Eric Tangumonkem, de su lucha con estos pensamientos y dudas. Dios lo llamó a América desde Camerún para realizar estudios de posgrado en la Universidad de Texas en Dallas, pero no tenía dinero para seguir este llamado. En este libro, Tangumonkem comparte su viaje de aprender a confiar en Dios cuando caminó en la fe y llegó a Estados Unidos a pesar de su falta de fondos. También comparte algunas de sus experiencias formativas previas a esta convocatoria-experiencias que estimularán a los lectores en su fe. La vida de Tangumonkem es un testimonio de la fidelidad de Dios, y él tiene cuidado en darle toda la.

MON ODYSSÉS AMÉRICAINE: UNE EXPÉRIENCE DE FOI (French Edition)

MON ODYSSÉE AMÉRICAINE: UNE EXPÉRIENCE DE FOI

ERIC TANGUMONKEM, Ph.D.

As-tu du mal à confier tes soucis financiers au Seigneur? Ressens-tu que Dieu t'appelle à faire quelque chose de grand, mais tu ne sais comment cela va se réaliser? Crains-tu qu'il va t'abandonner en chemin? Mon Odyssée Américaine: une expérience de foi est l'histoire d'Éric Tangumonkem et de sa lutte contre le doute et les pensées susmentionnées. Dieu l'a appelé depuis le Cameroun pour aller poursuivre ses études supérieures à l'Université du Texas à Dallas, mais il n'avait pas d'argent pour réaliser ce rêve. Dans ce livre, le Dr Tangumonkem partage avec vous les péripéties de son voyage qui l'ont amené à faire davantage confiance à Dieu alors qu'il se rendit aux États-Unis par la foi. Il partage également certaines des expériences qui l'ont bâti avant même son appel –expériences qui vont encourager les lecteurs dans leur foi. La vie du Dr Tangumonkem est un témoignage de la fidélité de Dieu à qui il rend toute la gloire.

God's Supernatural Agenda: 7 Secrets to Lasting Wealth and Prosperity

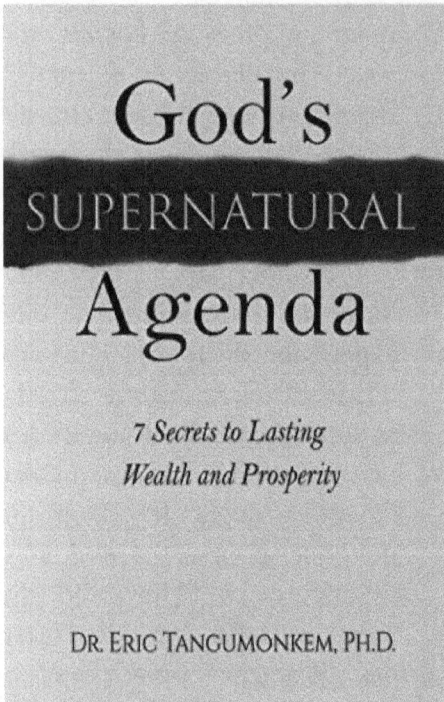

God's
SUPERNATURAL
Agenda

7 Secrets to Lasting
Wealth and Prosperity

DR. ERIC TANGUMONKEM, PH.D.

Is there something more valuable than money, precious stones, silver, and gold? Do you desire to be wealthy and prosperous? Are you already wealthy and prosperous, yet you feel empty and unsatisfied? Are you uncomfortable talking about money because it is "the root of all evil"? This book will not present shortcuts or get-rich-quick schemes, but important principles, laws, and processes involved in generating lasting wealth.

You see, God desires for ALL of us to prosper today and for all eternity. He has a divine reason for that desire, and He has given us the way to attain it. God's Supernatural Agenda: 7 Secrets to Lasting Wealth and Prosperity presents His blueprint for prosperity and explains why it is what truly matters.

Racism, Where Is Your Sting?
A provocative look at the beginning and the end of racism

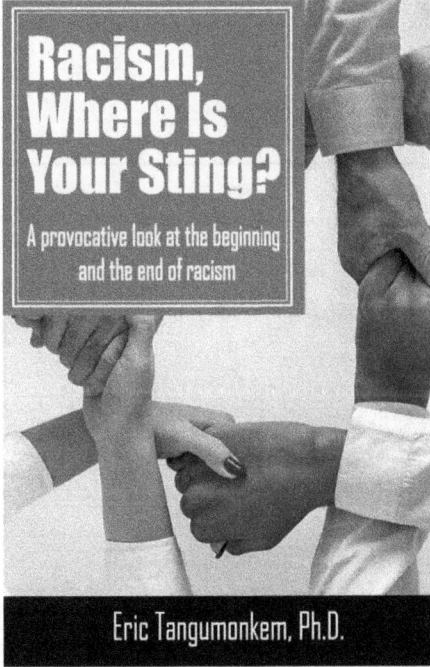

Each time the issue of racism is mentioned, tensions immediately run high, reason is thrown out the window, and emotional outbursts run rampant. Even though a lot of effort has been done to fight it, the devastating consequences continue to this day.

In this book, Dr. Tangumonkem challenges the status quo and presents a perspective that is both provocative and inspirational. Contrary to what you hear from those stoking the flames of racism and fermenting hate and bigotry, we are not at the mercy of racism. In fact, he dives deep into history to explain why the tendency to be racist is present in each one of us, regardless of skin color. The good news is that the victory has already been won — all we need is to live it out. When we stare right at this supercharged issue with fresh, unfiltered eyes, a seismic shift happens. Perhaps, the light at the end of racism is in sight.

IEM PRESS

To order additional copies of this book,
call 317-975-0806
or visit www.iempublishing.com

If you enjoyed this quality custom-published book,
drop by our website for more books and information.

"Inspiring, equipping, and motivating one author at a time."

www.ingramcontent.com/pod-product-compliance
Lightning Source LLC
Chambersburg PA
CBHW021128020426
42331CB00005B/675